Five Lectures on the American Civil War (1861–1865)

Five Lectures on the American Civil War (1861–1865)

Raimondo Luraghi
Translated from the Italian by Sean Mark

JOHN CABOT UNIVERSITY PRESS
Distributed by
UNIVERSITY OF DELAWARE PRESS

Published by John Cabot University Press
www.johncabot.edu

Distributed by University of Delaware Press
Co-published with The Rowman & Littlefield Publishing Group, Inc.
4501 Forbes Boulevard, Suite 200, Lanham, Maryland 20706
www.rowman.com

10 Thornbury Road, Plymouth PL6 7PP, United Kingdom

Copyright © 2013 by Raimondo Luraghi

All rights reserved. Authorization to photocopy item for internal or personal use, or the internal or personal use of specific clients, is granted by the copyright owner, provided that a base fee of $ 10.00, plus 8 cents per page, per copy is paid directly the copyright clearance center, 222 Rosewood Drive, Danvers, Massachusetts 01923.

British Library Cataloguing in Publication Information Available

Library of Congress Cataloging-in-Publication Data

Luraghi, Raimondo.
[Cinque lezioni sulla Guerra Civile americana (1861-1865). English] Five lectures on the American Civil War (1861-1865) / Raimondo Luraghi ; translated by Sean Mark.
pages cm
Includes bibliographical references.
ISBN 978-1-61149-426-6 (paper : alkaline paper)
1. United States--History--Civil War, 1861-1865. I. Title.
E468.L9513 2013
973.7--dc23
2012034224

The paper used in this publication meets the minimum requirements of American National Standard for Information Sciences Permanence of Paper for Printed Library Materials, ANSI/NISO Z39.48-1992.

Printed in the United States of America

Contents

Prefatory Note	vii
Note to English-Speaking Readers	ix
Note from the Translator	xi
I: Lecture I	1
II: Lecture II	13
III: Lecture III	25
IV: Lecture IV	37
V: Lecture V	51
Further Readings	63
Appendix	69
About the Author	71

Prefatory Note

This small volume is made up of the five lectures on the American Civil War (1861–1865) that I held some years ago at the Italian Institute for Philosophical Studies in Naples.

The reception they received in that city—truly an ideal place for the culture of the humanities, as well as the birthplace of Giambattista Vico, whom I have always considered my greatest mentor—encouraged me to revive them today, with the necessary and appropriate updates, and to dedicate my work to the illustrious memory of Vico.

As they are now, these five lectures are a further development of my almost forty-year study on the huge phenomenon that molded the modern American nation more than a century ago. They can provide a useful introduction to anyone who wishes to approach this fascinating topic, paving the way for further, more in-depth, readings.

I would like to thank here, for their multifaceted, good-natured help and exquisite courtesy, the board of the praiseworthy Italian Institute for Philosophic Studies, Avv. Gerardo Marotta and Prof. Antonio Gargano, and all their talented collaborators. Last but not least, I would like to thank my wife, Germana, for her encouragement and support during the writing of this small but dense volume.

Turin, November 9, 1996
Raimondo Luraghi

Note to English-Speaking Readers

The short essays presented here are the texts of five lectures delivered several years ago at the Istituto Italiano di Studi filosofici in Naples, published as *Cinque lezioni sulla guerra civile americana* (La Città del Sole, Naples, 1997). Naples is a city particularly devoted to history: it was in Naples that Giambattista Vico, the great philosopher of history, was born; there, too, the private library of Benedetto Croce is still visited by scholars and students. I would like to thank Prof. Antonio Gargano, director of the Istituto Italiano di Studi filosofici, for permission to publish this English translation.

I hope that English-speaking readers will find these lectures "neutral," whereas even today, many distinguished American colleagues are still divided between "federalists" and "confederates." Obviously, such a tragic event as the American Civil War cannot easily pass away from the memory of a whole people. Yet, the time seems ripe for a more impartial set of studies as I have tried to undertake.

The product of over thirty years of research on the American Civil War, this study synthetically analyzes the great drama that from 1861 to 1865 devastated the United States and gave rise to the modern American nation. The book also highlights how the Civil War was the first conflict of the industrial age and an often-neglected premonition of the two great wars that shook the world in the past century.

Raimondo Luraghi
Professor Emeritus, University of Genoa
Turin, March 17, 2012

Note from the Translator

The translator would like to thank Elizabeth Breiner for her insightful corrections.

I
Lecture I

The civil conflict that devastated the United States of America from 1861 to 1865 marks a pivotal period in the country's history, the importance and impact of which cannot be overestimated. Indeed, despite being hugely important events, the American Revolution and Independence did not radically alter the country's structure from a social, economic, and cultural perspective. And as for the French Revolution, this had very little influence on the history of North America.

The Civil War was, however, an entirely different matter, as it effectively buried "Old America" and deeply changed the country's structure, for both the winning and losing sides. Several states (covering roughly half of the Union) were compelled, "by blood and iron," to make the transition from the agrarian era to the great industrial era, and the Industrial Revolution, one of the triggering events behind the Civil War, spread victoriously throughout the entire country. The Union—previously, essentially an agglomeration of *disjecta membra*—was unified under conditions similar to those prevailing in Italy or, more fittingly, in Germany—and with the same methods.

As Europeans, we often tend to see the immense sprawl of the United States of America in a largely uniform way. As a result, too, of the Civil War's unification process, we are accustomed to thinking of the country as considerably more homogeneous than it really is—a belief that is starkly undermined if we look to the nation's past and origins. Indeed, it is remarkable just how heterogeneous the different states were, making it difficult to fathom how they were ever able to unify as a single nation (assuming this process of amalgamation has successfully occurred, something that, perhaps, should not be taken for granted).

European colonization of North America (or, rather, the part that today constitutes the United States) developed around a number of entirely unrelated centers, which were first reached by the Spanish. In 1525, with the permission of Emperor Charles V, Lucas Vázquez de Ayllón founded a colony on the coast of present-day South Carolina, bringing black slavery to North America for the very first time. When he died in 1527, the Spanish abandoned the colony, but the consequences of their presence proved lasting, as will later be discussed. Pánfilo de Nárvaez—Hernán Cortés's less fortunate rival—subsequently tried to enter the country through the Gulf of Mexico. His expedition failed and cost him his life, but he paved the way for another colonizer who made a much greater impact on history, Hernando de Soto. Passing through Florida, he successfully reached what are now the states of Georgia and Alabama and discovered the Mississippi River, before dying on its banks in 1542.

Florida had already been explored (and given its name) by Juan Ponce de Léon in 1513, and, in 1565, after exterminating a colony of French Huguenots, Pedro Menéndez de Avilés founded the town of San Agustin there. This was the first town to be built by European settlers in North America, and the grace of the Spanish colonial architecture is still visible today.

After the Spanish explorers passed through Florida and Georgia, religious missions began to appear and multiply throughout these territories, with Spanish Jesuits reaching as far north as Virginia. These missions became local centers of work and learning. Under the direction of the monks, the natives—who had been converted, more or less successfully, to Catholicism—would farm the land, build dams and channels, rear livestock, do simple brickwork, and perform various types of handicraft. The missions were self-sufficient units and produced enough to meet the needs and requirements of community life. It would certainly be interesting to explore how much of this tradition contributed to the genesis, in the following centuries, of another self-sufficient unit, the unique institution of the Southern plantation.

The Spanish settlers permanently modified the flora and fauna of what later became the Southern United States. From Europe, they brought vegetables and crops (such as corn), as well as farmyard animals and horses, and began growing tobacco.

French colonizers (with the exception of the aforementioned Huguenot colony in Florida, which left its trace in place names such as Beaufort and Port Royal) reached the South from Canada, which they had begun colonizing in 1534—ten years after Giovanni da Verrazzano had explored the coasts of North America on behalf of the French king, François I. French settlers explored and colonized the Mississippi valley in the seventeenth century, founding the city of New Orleans at the mouth of the river, capital of the great colony they named Louisiana in honor of Louis XIV, the Sun King. By that point, French and Spanish settlers had profoundly influenced what was later to become the South, embedding Creole culture in various forms and substantially and permanently altering the region's prospects in terms of agriculture and livestock.

English colonization in North America further accentuated the differences between the various regions. This was an inevitable process, given the very particular characteristics of English presence in the New World.

The Tudor monarchy in England had been established after the War of the Roses had virtually destroyed the great feudal nobility and deprived it of all political influence. Royal power had its foundations, of course, in the merchant and banking bourgeoisie of the city of London but also (and to a greater extent) a lower and upper landowning aristocracy, which found political representation in the House of Lords and provided the king with county lieutenants, curators of the judicial archives, and all the members of the government. The lower strata of this nobility consisted in a tight-knit group of country squires, or country gentlemen, who shared a great number of aspirations with the lords: "to acquire status, judicial functions in local courts, become patron of the parish, perform paternalistic duties toward those of an inferior social rank, and ultimately embark on a political career, become a member of the House of Commons and in some cases (who knows?) even a nobleman, a Lord, a baronet" (Raimondo Luraghi, *Gli Stati Uniti* [The United States], Turin, 1974).

Below them on the social ladder were the yeomen, a class made up of free men who owned their own farms. In short, society was agrarian in nature, and its members had aspirations and ideals of an eminently pre-capitalist nature. There was, however, no disdain for trade—and, without realizing it, society was already unable to exist autonomously, without the capitalist market where its products, predominantly wool, were sold.

It is worth adding that very many of these yeomen had become wealthy through the expropriation and sale of the clergy's assets, carried out by King Henry VIII after the Anglican schism, and, for this reason, they were inextricably linked to the fate of the monarchy.

This society reached its peak during the reign of the energetic and farsighted Elizabeth I. At this time, the cultural wave of the Renaissance from Italy was striking England in full, and Italian had become the language spoken by the cultured members of society, who also had a sound knowledge of Latin. Even the English language was undergoing a Latinate transformation, with the introduction of vocabulary and syntactical constructions of Latin origin. The ideals pursued by this aristocratic class had been eloquently and readily provided by Baldassare Castiglione in his *Book of the Courtier*. According to Castiglione, gentlemen should not lend themselves to the activities of the "vile marchaunt" but, rather, to the pursuit of glory (and wealth acquired gloriously), and where better to find this than in the remote lands of the New World? As Sir Walter Raleigh, Castiglione's mentor, eloquently put it, gentlemen should strive:

>   To seeke New Worlds,
>   For golde, for prayse, for glory.

Identifying with these ideals, an expedition in 1603 founded the colony that Raleigh had already named Virginia in honor of Queen Elizabeth and was destined to become the ideological and political center of the South.

The first Europeans who came to the American coasts to found colonies had their heads full of classical ideals, as shown in Peter Martyr d'Anghiera's *Decades of the New World*. The author describes the first contacts and Spanish conquests in the New World in Virgilian tones, drawing comparison with the arrival of Aeneas in the lands of Turnus and Latinus. The *Decades* had been translated into English in 1555 by Richard Eden, causing quite a stir, and in 1556, the third volume of Giovan Battista Ramusio's *Of the Navigations and Voyages*, devoted to the Americas, was translated into English.

This classical take on the New World, alongside the agrarian ideal of the Elizabethan gentleman, would thus have proved profoundly influential in the foundation of the first English colonial nucleus in Virginia. The remnants, too, of Spanish and French settlements throughout the South would also have had an influential impact. In Virginia, certainly, the climate was mild, the land fertile, abundant, and available, and the mentality of the settlers suited to give rise to an aristocratic and agrarian society, in imitation of the Elizabethan example in Britain.

That the first settlers were generally people of quite modest social status, rather than gentlemen, is largely irrelevant, as the figure of the agrarian gentleman was an ideal to aspire to, a model to imitate, the height of their desires. In this sense, Sir Walter Raleigh can legitimately be considered the ideal figure on which the new gentleman modeled himself, and although Raleigh never made it to Virginia, the historian Marshall Fishwick quite rightly puts him first in his list of *Gentlemen of Virginia*.

African American slavery was introduced in Virginia very early on, as early as 1619, by Dutch and British merchants who thrived on the slave trade. Slavery was already present in all the colonies in the Americas, and the first to bring slaves to that continent were probably the Portuguese in Brazil. The slave-labor system (which was then accepted as normal) accentuated the agrarian nature of the Southern colonies, as did the colonial practice of headrights, the widespread system whereby fifty acres of land were guaranteed to those settlers who brought their families with them. This contributed enormously to the South's agrarian, individualistic, and decentralized social structure and certainly did not encourage urban development.

The origins of colonial settlements in the North were very different. In 1620, a small vessel called the Mayflower left English shores for America. On board was a group of British emigrants who, two centuries later, would become known as the Pilgrim Fathers, though they themselves would never know it. After exploring the coast, on the December 11, they landed in what is now Massachusetts. There, in a bay surrounded by hills, they founded a new city and called it New Plymouth. A decade later, around 1630, other settlers followed suit, later known as the Puritans—a name that they themselves used.

In England, the Tudor line failed with the death of Elizabeth I in 1603, and the crown passed to the Stuart dynasty of James I. The first problem the king found himself facing was precisely that of Puritanism. Under his predecessors, the term had been applied generically to all those who sought to reform the Anglican Church in a more strictly Protestant sense: namely, with a transition from schism to reformation. Despite being a fairly composite ensemble, the most influential group was certainly the Calvinists, also known as the Presbyterians, who wanted to remove Episcopal authority and replace it with elected representative bodies, in addition to appointing an elected central body, made up of pastors and lay people. Alongside the Calvinists were the Congregationalists, who wanted each congregation to be autonomous, without a central body of any kind.

Despite its internal distinctions, Puritanism had a well-defined ideological outline. The Puritans considered themselves the elect of God, as they had seen the "light" of "real" religion; all those who were unable to see it formed the great mass of reprobates—hence, the enemies of God—over which the elect would inevitably triumph. The Puritan doctrine was extremely militant in nature, and with the certainty that they had been chosen by God came a complete belief in their destiny, an attitude that would have formidable impact when the time came to fight.

In terms of social background, the Puritans came predominantly from the nascent bourgeois classes, mainly devoted to trade, craft manufacturing, and banking; they were driven by an authentic religious inspiration, which was, however, very well suited to their economic interests. The elect few believed it their duty to work tirelessly, produce, and save money, and their earnings were a just reward from God. The Puritan attitude toward the poor was singularly devoid of charity: according to their doctrine, poverty was the rightful punishment that God reserved for idlers and nonbelievers.

With these sorts of ideas, the Puritans would have evidently struggled to coexist with both the Anglican Church (which they considered as deeply satanic as Counter-Reformation "papism") and the absolutist Stuart monarchy—especially since James I did not share Elizabeth's conciliatory attitude and talent for smoothing things over and showed little propensity for overseas expansion. Thus, many Puritans decided to leave England for the unknown shores of America. Imbued with Old Testament doctrine, they saw the kingdom of Britain as the "slavery of Babylon" from which they had to break free in order to reach the new "promised land." There, they would found the "city on the hill" and establish St. Augustine's concept of the *civitas Dei*, having abandoned the *civitas diaboli* of the British Isles and Europe.

As has been rightly pointed out, theirs was an attempt to escape history by taking refuge in a utopian fantasy. The colonies they founded and called New England were, however, destined to have enormous consequences on the entire history of America. Centuries later, an eminent Southerner remarked that the Puritans had fled Europe in search of freedom and had immediately begun to take away everyone else's, once they had arrived in the New World. Indeed, the Puritan doctrine only contemplated freedom *within the group*, and, in Connecticut, one of the New England colonies, a law was even passed whereby anyone who did not follow the "true religion" should be put to death. Those among them who did not accept such fanaticism had no choice but to emigrate with Pastor Roger Williams, who founded the small colony of Rhode Island.

The first to suffer the consequences of this doctrine were the Native Americans or, as they were then called, the Indians. In the religious myth create by the Puritans, the Native Americans played the biblical part of the Philistines, the Canaanites, and the Amalekites; what else could the elect do but exterminate them? Naturally, they could not be converted, as the Native Americans were evil—the devil—and converting the devil is evidently impossible. The ferocious Puritan fanaticism soon began to seek out new enemies, both abroad (in the French "papists") and internally (with the horrendous witchcraft trials).

Nothing could have been more different from the atmosphere prevailing in the colony of Virginia, on the one hand, and New England, on the other. Even further differentiating the two, the Puritan system of colonization was not founded on the individualism of the *headrights* system (as it was in Virginia) but on the *township* system, whereby the land was divided and split up into groups intended for development into urban nuclei; consequently, civilization in New England was resolutely urban and bourgeois in nature, as opposed to the agricultural, individualistic, and rural organization of the South.

Slavery did not spread in New England; rather, it died out almost immediately. As a working system, it was ill fitted to merchant trading and craft manufacturing. To make up for this, the Puritans of New England, whose economy depended largely on sea trade, began instead to deal in slaves, reaping enormous profits. Thus, when the colony of Virginia—gravely concerned by the huge influx of African slaves that this trade was causing—decreed that the slave trade be made illegal, the Puritans persuaded London to cancel these provisions, arguing that the slave trade was far too lucrative to renounce.

The colonies that subsequently arose in the North and South conformed, by and large, to these initial models, though they often maintained certain differences. Generally, in the Northern colonies, the ideological fanaticism of New England was either muted (as occurred in New York) or entirely rejected (as was the case with Pennsylvania); however, socially and economically, these colonies greatly resembled New England, both in the social background of their founders and in their geographical characteristics, which encouraged manufacture, trade, handicraft, and banking. In the South, the mild climate, poor port system, and abundance of good, fertile land favored the spread of the economic model of Virginia, as well as slavery. Indigo, tobacco, and rice prospered, while cotton was still scarcely cultivated in the colonial era. Short-staple cotton could not be used, as the fiber broke when the cotton was stripped, and long-staple cotton could thrive only in the sandy soils of the coastal islands of South Carolina and Georgia; for this reason, this valuable but scarce variety was known as "sea islands" cotton. In the seventeenth century, two surveyors, Charles Mason and Jeremiah Dixon, who had been commissioned to mark the boundary between Pennsylvania and Maryland, drew the line that took their name and became, from then onward, the border between North and South.

In the second half of the eighteenth century, Britain's complete disregard for the needs of the American settlers succeeded in uniting all thirteen colonies against it in the War of Independence. Once the United States were constituted, however, it did not take long for the differences to reemerge. The rich landowning classes of the agrarian South were accustomed, as aristocratic classes often are, to engage in political and military activity. The majority of the leaders in the fight against Britain—from George Washington and Thomas Jefferson to Patrick Henry—had come from this class; indeed, Virginia produced four of the five earliest presidents of the United States. They formed an enlightened and politically moderate elite, who believed collaboration should be encouraged in the nascent United States between the North and South—granting the South political control, while giving the North economic and financial leadership of the Union.

Very quickly, however, this delicate balance fell through, as the secretary of the treasury, Alexander Hamilton of New York, adopted a policy of strict centralization. Among other things, this led to the disbanding of the Federalist Party (which had led the way in the constitutional process) and the formation, in opposition to the Federalists, of the Democratic Party, which was founded and led by a Southerner, Thomas Jefferson. Eventually, a compromise was reached, but, in the political struggle, Jefferson issued a set of political statements that spoke volumes about the political ideology of the South: the Kentucky and Virginia Resolutions of 1798 and 1799. The resolutions bluntly state "that the several states composing the United States of America are not united on the principle of unlimited submission to their general government," and that each state is reserved the right to declare void any laws and regulations passed by the national government that appear to flagrantly harm the state's interests.

The documents thus assert that the United States was, in fact, an inhomogeneous group of independent and sovereign states, with all the implications that this entailed.

The North's response was swift. In 1812, war had broken out against Britain, and, in 1814, the New England states, which opposed the continuation of the fighting, held a meeting in Connecticut, known as the Hartford Convention, to discuss a potential secession from the Union. The threat fell through when the war came to an end, but the rallying cry of secession had been launched. It is true that the slogan never truly suited such a strongly centralist faction, but it is also true that the South's adoption of it against the North was not unexpected.

The reason why the New England states (with the tacit support of the entire North) had opposed the war so vehemently was that their economies relied heavily on merchant trading, and trade with Britain proved the most lucrative. During the war, however, trade had been heavily restricted, as the Royal Navy blockaded much of the American coastline. Some historians believe that it was precisely this embargo that encouraged the rise of a new, local industry in the North of the United States, particularly in the textile sector. The Northern bourgeoisie thus began to change from a predominantly mercantile and free-trading class to a more industrial and protectionist one.

The Industrial Revolution had long since exploded and triumphed in Britain, and it now began to take hold in America. The demand for cotton on the world market had increased enormously, and the South had the right land, climate, and manpower to meet it. In 1797, Eli Whitney had invented a machine that could process short-staple cotton without breaking the fiber. This machine would have probably been remembered as little more than a curious invention if the world market had not suddenly shown an unrestrained hunger for cotton. All of a sudden, the South began to discard tobacco and indigo cultivation in favor of the new commodity, and cotton production rose from 3,816,600 kilograms in 1796 to 46,535,000 kilograms in 1816. The greatest Southern statesman of those years, John Caldwell Calhoun, from South Carolina, foresaw the possibility of reconciling North and South, with the South providing the raw materials for the North's nascent cotton industry. Therefore, as the transformation from mercantile to industrial gradually took place, the North abandoned free trade and asked for protective tariffs, in response to which Calhoun proposed a moderate duty to assist the region with its economic shift.

The political repercussions of these social changes were significant: in the presidential elections of 1820, James Monroe, the Democratic Party candidate from Virginia, was elected almost unanimously. The Federalist Party had collapsed, and, for a brief time, the United States had the rather unique experience of legally and democratically being a country under single-party rule. This was the so-called Era of Good Feelings, which predictably underwent a rapid downfall.

The Industrial Revolution was swiftly gaining momentum in the North, and the moderate protectionist measures proposed by Calhoun no longer appeared sufficient to many. Senator Henry Clay called for a strong tariff increase, suggesting that the government of the Union use the proceeds to finance a vast campaign of public works to improve and facilitate industry and trade in the North (developing its means of communication canals, ports, etc.). The South reacted negatively, arguing that it was effectively being made to pay for the North's industrialization, as cotton was the only product keeping the trade balance active, and the protective tariffs were forcing Southerners to buy Northern products, which were more expensive than the British or French equivalents and of inferior quality. Was the South not being reduced to the status of a semicolony?

For the moment, however, this was not yet a widespread cause for alarm in the South. Instead, at that time, a plan for the emancipation of slaves was being prepared, and in the 1820s, with the endorsement of President Monroe, the American Colonization Society was founded. The society planned to buy vast plots of land in Africa and resettle freed slaves there, providing them with agricultural property. This was the origin of the Liberian state: a noble initiative, albeit an entirely utopian one.

Nevertheless, tensions between the North and South reached a point at which direct conflict could no longer be avoided. On February 13, 1819, while Congress was debating the admission of Missouri as a state, New York representative John Tallmadge proposed a resolution whereby Missouri would be accepted as a state of the Union on the condition that slavery be abolished therein. This proposal had an explosive effect in the House of Representatives; Congress had never contended directly with the issue of slavery before. Throughout the Union, it was customarily considered an institution of private law and, therefore, left in the hands of individual states. In those years, the North had shown very little concern about slavery, as it was considered largely at odds with the interests and lives of that section of the country. In the South, philanthropic societies prospered, seeking ways to improve the condition of slaves, with the ultimate goal of emancipating them and abolishing the institution of slavery. Why, then, would a representative of New York raise such a contentious issue in Congress?

The fact of the matter was that, in the years preceding Tallmadge's resolution, there had been an ever-increasing impetus for westward expansion. The Midwest was predominantly inhabited by peasants and free farmers, who were, traditionally, political allies of the South, united by shared agrarian interests. However, the South argued that a ban on slavery in Missouri, and—by extension—the other sizeable Western territories, would discriminate against farmers of the slaveholding states, who would thus be discouraged from moving to the new territories, which would instead be reserved solely for Midwestern farmers. At any rate, the resolution would grant Midwestern farmers privileged access to the territories, while also creating a point of radical divergence with their former political allies of the South. The policy was, in other words, a very able attempt to break the agrarian alliance and politically isolate the South.

The reaction of the South can be better understood if viewed in the context of the restlessness that was spreading within it. For quite some time, the region had been losing its political authority, and immigrants from Europe, repelled by the presence of slavery and unable to compete with slave labor, were increasingly taking leave of the South. The population there remained stable but was diminishing in relation to the North's, which was growing rapidly. Calhoun's attempt to reach an agreement with the North by introducing a moderate protective tariff had failed: the North remained protectionist and hostile and kept demanding more.

These conditions ultimately led to a very bitter clash in Congress. Showing great moderation and breadth of political views, the Southerners eventually agreed to compromise on what became known as the Missouri Compromise of 1820. There would be no prohibition on slavery in the state of Missouri, but from that moment onward, the "peculiar institution" of slavery would be banned in all lands above the line of 36 degrees 30 minutes north latitude, that is, the southern border of the new state of Missouri. With this act, the Southerners demonstrated their willingness to accept a smaller part of the immense territory that Thomas Jefferson had purchased from France in the Louisiana Purchase of 1803. The land in question was very fertile and, geographically speaking, formed something like a vast inverted triangle, with New Orleans at the tip and the Canadian border as the base; it also included the entire Mississippi valley, right up to the Rocky Mountains, beyond which lay the Spanish (and later Mexican) territories of California. It went without saying that, under the Missouri Compromise, the vast majority of these immense lands would remain open to Midwestern farmers, with whom, for the time being, the South was able to reinforce its political alliance.

Nevertheless, Tallmadge's attempt to isolate the South had exposed how potentially dangerous such policies could be. The time had not been right for attempting to implement such policies—but the effort had undoubtedly brought to light a potential cause for concern among Southerners. Thomas Jefferson, whose long life was by then drawing to a close, sensed this clearly, writing in a letter that the Missouri controversy had echoed in his ear like "a fire bell in the night"—the early warning of a deadly crisis to come, which might one day bring about the demise of the Union.

In the years following the Missouri Compromise, the "Era of Good Feelings" (or good intentions) completely collapsed, and the protectionists and conservatives in the North broke away from the Democratic Party to form a new political grouping: the National Republican Party, also known as the Whigs. Thus began the Second Party System, with the rival parties of the Democrats and Whigs replacing the dualistic antagonism of Democrats and Federalists.

Also in those years, the Industrial Revolution was picking up momentum at a tremendous speed throughout the United States, explaining the North's complete conversion to protectionism. This was characterized—following European example—by three factors: (a) production was mechanized through the use of machinery on a large scale, leading to a staggering increase in the quantity of goods produced; (b) new and, so to speak, artificial energy sources were increasingly employed, as previously used sources of natural energy—such as wind, falling water and animal traction—were replaced and made redundant by the steam engine; (c) production became mass production, and a large industrial proletariat was formed.

The novelty was that, in these industrial societies, agriculture was subordinate to industry, as was the countryside to the city. This was unlike what had occurred in agricultural societies up until that point (and continued to happen in the South), where the land was the center of production and the manufacturing industry subordinate to it, with the industry functioning predominantly—perhaps exclusively—to meet the needs of the prevailing agricultural activity.

This reality had now been turned on its head, as the agrarian community was being increasingly reduced to mere supplier of raw materials and foodstuffs for the urban industries. In its relations with the North, the South was slowly assuming the role of a vast rural expanse that was subordinate to an equally impressive urban reality. However reluctantly, the South had to adapt to the North's ever-increasing demands.

In 1827, delegates from thirteen Northern states, assembled in Harrisburg, Pennsylvania, put forward a clear demand for higher protective tariffs; on May 13, 1828, Congress responded by establishing an ad valorem duty of 45 percent. Anger erupted in the South. John Calhoun, by now the South's undisputed leader, wished to defend the interests of his section of the country, while also avoiding escalating tensions to a certain breaking point. Thus, on December 19, the South Carolina legislature issued a document of protest, also known as Calhoun's Exposition, in which he reiterated, expanded, and clarified the Jeffersonian doctrine of nullification—namely, that, within their borders, states had the right to reject any federal laws that were seen to damage their legitimate interests.

However, in 1832, the new president, Andrew Jackson—a Southern Democrat from a lower-middle-class background, hostile to Southern planters, and a firm upholder of the authority of the central government—renewed the protective tariffs, introducing only a slight reduction, which seemed all but laughable to the South. On November 19, 1832, the South Carolina legislature applied the theories put forward in its 1828 doctrine and declared the tariff null and void. In retaliation, Jackson sent warships to collect duties on the high seas off the coasts of South Carolina. Finally, a compromise was reached: the tariffs would be halved by 1834.

What, then, was the outcome of the political struggle? The South had undoubtedly lost, although it had managed to avoid being utterly undone. Although the duties of protection remained, the North was made to realize that it was still a long way off from being able to impose its laws and duties on the South at will. On the other hand, South Carolina was left politically isolated by its protest against the central government, as no other Southern state had dared to follow suit, despite the fact that they were all adversely affected by the tariffs. In any case, direct confrontation had been postponed, as, for the time being, the Midwest's alliance with the South held strong, with common agrarian interests still prevailing over sectional differences.

Very significantly, the two sections had set out their ideological principles clearly during the debates held in Congress. According to Daniel Webster of Massachusetts, the Union took precedence over the individual states; its powers did not derive from the states but from the American people. For this reason, he believed nullification was unacceptable, almost treason. Calhoun replied that the United States were not a nation but a union of independent and sovereign states; thus, legislation and final authority ultimately rested with the state. The two positions could not have been more irreconcilable.

II

Lecture II

By the 1840s, the Industrial Revolution had changed the face of America. On the great rivers of the West, steamboats were replacing the rafts used by the pioneers; on land, the railroad network was in continual expansion, and its 5,324 kilometers had stretched to an incredible 50,000 kilometers by 1860. The changes to American life brought about by the railways, however, were not merely quantitative in nature. The Midwest, long-standing ally of the South, was no longer only connected to the sea by the Mississippi River and the port of New Orleans, as the railroad provided a direct connection to the Atlantic through the ports of New York, New England, and Pennsylvania.

These changes in communications quickly undermined the strategy adopted by the Democratic Party, which was dependent upon the converging interests of the farmers in the South and the Midwest to isolate the bourgeois and capitalistic North. But what eventually brought the situation to tipping point, causing the latent tensions between Southerners and Midwesterners to erupt, began as a demographic issue.

As mentioned above, migrants from Europe had typically chosen to settle in the Northern states, where they would not face competition from slave labor. This was yet to have a serious impact, however, as immigration rates were still relatively low in the early decades of the nineteenth century.

The European crisis of the 1840s and, in particular, the wave of repression that followed the 1848 Revolutions changed matters, and migration to America suddenly and dramatically increased. In 1849, 207,024 immigrants crossed the Atlantic, rising to 310,004 in 1850 and 439,442 in 1851. From then onward, migrants flocked to the country at an average rate of 200,000 a year and settled almost entirely in the Northern states. Fortunately, in the early years of the Industrial Revolution, America, unlike Europe, had a safety valve preventing mass unemployment from spreading in its burgeoning industry's need for an "industrial reserve army" made up of unemployed workers. The expansion caused by the boom in industry and population was, however, restricted by the frontier, the vast land to the west that was yet to be colonized. All of a sudden, the question of state-owned land became a very pressing issue for the Union, as the entire West was considered national property, pending the reaching of the population quorum for new states to be formed. The route of migratory expansion was thus to be forged through the agricultural states of the Midwest.

The enormous social upheaval and sudden increase in population due to mass immigration gave rise to two new political movements of serious consequence. The first was the party of the Nativists, more commonly known as the Know Nothings, known as such because it resembled a secret society and was unwilling to disclose its real objectives. The party incited widespread hostility toward the newly arrived migrants, the "non-Americans," and its members shared anti-Catholic sentiments (as many immigrants, such as the Irish, were Catholic) as well as anti-Southern ones (as they were hostile to African Americans, both freemen and slaves).

The second party was the Free Soil Party, which was of much greater political consequence. The Free Soilers adopted a blunt stance on slavery, arguing that it should be abolished in the Western territories, which should instead accommodate free, white farmers. The political program of the Free Soil Party was set out clearly by one of the most eminent Midwestern Free Soilers, Abraham Lincoln, of Illinois, who stated in a public speech that the territories were to be reserved for "free white people."

The Free Soilers essentially wanted to keep slave owners out of the West in order to keep out the black population, who (as slaves or—even worse—as freemen) would have created competition for the possession of the lands, as well as the labor on them. It is important to bear in mind that the Free Soil Party—unlike the Nativists—did not have a specific political structure but rather found its consensus cutting across the larger, more established political parties.

The agricultural Midwestern states were the bulwark of the Free Soilers, and not only was this upsetting the Midwest's traditional alliance with the South, but also it was placing it on a collision course with the very same Southern states that, up until then, it had considered its political allies.

This conflict had dramatically first emerged in the Mexican-American War of 1846. Texas had gained its independence in 1836, but Mexico had never truly accepted its independent status, and conflict had once again broken out. This time, however, the United States also joined the quarrel, as Texas had asked to join the Union. That same year, in the U.S. Congress, the Free Soiler David Wilmot had suggested a proviso whereby slavery would be prohibited in all the new territories that had been taken from Mexico, with the exception of Texas. Wilmot was a Democrat, and his proposal dramatically divided the members of Democratic Party politically, if not yet physically.

The Wilmot Proviso unambiguously revealed what the Free Soilers were hoping to achieve: the complete exclusion of the Southerners from the Western territories. This caused great alarm to spread throughout the entire South, which consequently descended into a state of panic.

To better understand the South's extreme reaction, we must bear in mind that the population in the North and Midwest was growing continuously—predominantly as a result of the massive migration from Europe—while in the South, it remained stable. This had political implications in the House of Representatives, as each state was permitted a number of representatives that was directly proportional to its population—meaning the South had been the minority for a long time. In the Senate, where there were fourteen states on either side, the South still maintained a precarious balance, but this would be tipped as soon as Free Soil states began to crop up in the Western territories. The South saw the proviso as the first step toward turning it into a political minority, which, they feared, would initially be tolerated and later trampled.

Southern fears were heightened by a movement that had meanwhile sprung up in the North calling for the complete and immediate abolition of slavery, and accompanying its requests was a series of scathing attacks on the Southerners, whom they saw as inhumane and sinful. Societies for the abolition of slavery had in fact originated in the South between the 1820s and 1830s, seeking ways to eliminate the "peculiar institution," which was seen as a disgrace. In 1832 and 1834, an act to abolish slavery had even been proposed in the Virginia and Tennessee legislatures and was narrowly defeated by a few votes.

The defeat was due to a number of factors. Firstly—although a large number of Southerners, perhaps even the majority, were adverse to slavery as an institution—slave labor had become an essential part of cotton production. The Industrial Revolution in Europe had created a huge demand for cotton on the global market, and Eli Whitney's invention of the cotton gin had made the commodity more readily available. Secondly, a sudden and irrevocable change in social relations in the South might have led to the collapse of the entire production system, with disastrous consequences.

At most, these two motives would have delayed the process of emancipation, and made it more gradual (which was probably the only way it could have occurred without a devastating social shake-up). Although many influential Southerners held onto their conviction that slavery should be abolished and said so openly, all talk of emancipation was eventually put to one side, but this was due to an entirely different reason.

Nineteenth-century liberal culture by then found the institution of slavery, which had been deemed natural in previous centuries, to be no longer acceptable. In 1834, under the impetus of William Wilberforce's campaigning,

Britain had gradually freed approximately 700,000 black slaves through compensation in its West Indian colonies.

Britain's example had urged two brothers from New York, Arthur and Lewis Tappan, to found the American Anti-Slavery Society, which also called for progressive emancipation. The Bostonian William Lloyd Garrison, founder in 1831 of the newspaper the *Liberator*, adopted an even more radical stance. With the vigorous intransigence typical of New England, he denounced slavery from a moral point of view, seeing it as a fault, a sin, which should be immediately abolished, with complete disregard for the "sinners," who should be justly punished. Garrison went so far as to suggest that the Northern states secede from the Union so they would no longer have to associate with the "sinners" in the South.

Despite causing quite a stir, abolitionists in the North remained a minority without political influence. Their incessant propaganda campaign (which, in itself, had been enough to frighten the South) was, however, heavily reinforced when it received the backing of the Free Soil movement. The Free Soilers were by no means abolitionists; if anything, with the odd exception, they were hostile to the black population, fearing that once slave owners were admitted to the Western territories, they would free their slaves, who would create undesirable competition for labor. But despite the distinctly racist elements of its program, the Free Soil Party was a mass movement, with far more political following than the abolitionists, and this made them very threatening and dangerous in the eyes of the South.

Seen together, these factors accounted for the widespread climate of anxiety, resentment, and alarm in the South. With its increasingly clear attempts to turn the South into an economic colony, the North was seen as an oppressive presence, a kind of *Hannibal ante portas*. It was this impending threat that had led the South to set aside any talk of emancipating its slaves (with its more enlightened citizens hoping this was only a temporary measure).

Unfortunate events seemed to keep coming thick and fast. What was to be done with the Western territories? The Wilmot Proviso had reached a stalemate in Congress, with the South determined not to concede. What, then, was to be done? Some suggested that the Missouri line be extended to the Pacific Ocean, but this was impossible for at least two reasons. First of all, the Missouri Compromise concerned the lands acquired through the Louisiana Purchase and not those lying below them, which had been obtained from Mexico.

Secondly, in 1848, gold had been discovered in California. Ironically, the Spanish conquistadores, who had breathlessly sought the precious metal for centuries, had literally been walking on the stuff for years, without realizing it. From its initial discovery, gold caused political disruption within the Union. Drawn to the mirage of wealth, large numbers of men headed west (50,000 in 1849 alone), and the population of sleepy California grew exponentially. With the gold hunters came bands of adventurers, profiteers, desperadoes, and bandits of all sorts; and the settlers of California decided to take advantage of this increase in population to found the state of California, with its own constitution in which (as good Free Soilers) slavery was prohibited. The Republic of California, with its own antislavery constitution, thus came knocking at the door of Congress, asking to be admitted to the Union. Extending the Missouri line to the Pacific, therefore, became impossible, as doing so would cut California in two. The situation reached fever pitch.

The only thing keeping the crisis from boiling over was that all the parties involved were not prepared to take any irreparable steps. Also, the respected "old guard" of the Senate—Henry Clay, Daniel Webster, and John Calhoun—was still very much alive and carried a great deal of influence. Clay and Webster laid down the conditions for a new compromise: California would be admitted to the Union, with its own constitution prohibiting slavery, but in the remainder of the territories taken from Mexico, legislation regarding slavery would be left to the future states arising therein. The slave trade would be made illegal in the federal district containing the capital, and the Fugitive Slave Law would be passed, stating that slaves who had fled to the North were to be pursued and returned to their masters.

John Calhoun did not support the compromise. By the time it reached debate in the Senate, he was a dying man. He nevertheless turned up in the chamber, though he did not have the strength to read his speech, which was read by another senator. In it, Calhoun (who strongly opposed the war against Mexico, fearing—and rightly so—the potential political fallout following the subdivision of the newly acquired territories) rejected the compromise, illustrating how it merely deferred the problems, rather than resolving them. He saw the Fugitive Slave Law as an attempt to pull the wool over the eyes of the people, as very few slaves actually fled to the North, and believed that the law would have put the Southerners in an unflattering light before the Northerners and the rest of the world. Furthermore, it would have been largely impossible for Southern slave owners to reclaim their fugitive slaves against the will of local Northern communities.

Calhoun instead proposed a sort of Austro Hungarian Compromise, consisting in the formation of two separate but associated Unions, which shared only foreign policy and defense. Calhoun was convinced (though he did not say so in his speech) that if the country took the path of compromise proposed by Clay and Webster, it would lead to secession, civil war, and the South's undoing.

Nevertheless, Congress voted in favor of the Compromise of 1850, and tensions began to ease, until, toward the end of 1851, a little-known newspaper, the *National Era*, began to publish installments of a novel called *Uncle Tom's Cabin*, later to appear in book form the following year. Although it remains a masterpiece of popular fiction, the book was entirely detached from the reality of the South, and the author herself confessed that she had no real firsthand knowledge of the South or slavery. In the inflamed climate of the 1850s, however, the book added fuel to the fire. Tens of thousands of copies were sold, and several stage adaptations followed, in which the depiction of the South was, if anything, even more rough-hewn.

As unrest grew, a problem was brewing in Kansas and Nebraska, as both advanced the request to become territories (which was only possible once a certain population was reached). As these lands were part of the Louisiana Purchase and stood north of the 36°30' line, it seemed obvious that they should be subjected to the provisions of the Missouri Compromise. The trouble was that, in the heated climate following the California question and the publication of *Uncle Tom's Cabin*, the thought of having a Free Soil state to the west—along with those in the north and the east—had the Missourians trembling and ready to do anything to prevent it.

To prevent (or at least delay) the conflicting interests of the South and the Midwest from causing a disastrous split within the Democratic Party, the new party leader, Senator Stephen Douglas of Illinois, proposed a bill that was approved in 1854, the Kansas-Nebraska Act. The bill stated that it was the settlers in those territories—rather than the future states that would later be founded therein—who should determine through popular sovereignty whether slavery was to be permitted within each territory.

Douglas hoped that, in this way, Kansas would go to the Southerners and Nebraska to the Free Soilers. He had not considered, however, that much of the local population was actually largely undecided. At this point, hordes of both pro-slavery and antislavery settlers flooded to Kansas from North and South, to try and swing the vote. Kansas was thus left with two territorial legislatures, two provisional constitutions—and a civil war.

Meanwhile, a new party had entered the fray, also riding the wave of unrest in Kansas. It was made up of former Whigs and Democrats and brought together Free Soilers, conservatives, protectionists, and abolitionists. The Republican Party was its name, and it looked like the first political party potentially capable of unifying the entire North, with all its disparate ideas, on the basis of an anti-Southern sentiment.

Tensions continued to mount, as a quarrel in the Senate in 1856 perfectly illustrates. In his address, Senator Charles Sumner, an anti-Southern Republican, violently attacked the aging Senator Butler of South Carolina, insulting him in offensive tones, which he certainly did not deserve. The gesture was ugly and out of place; much worse, however, was the response of Representative Preston Brooks, nephew of Senator Butler, who sought to defend his uncle's honor by savagely beating Sumner over the head with a cane in the middle of the Senate chamber, to the point of almost killing him.

This was the climate in which the presidential elections took place that year. Although he was defeated, the newly formed Republican Party candidate, explorer John C. Frémont, received 114 electoral votes against the 174 received by the victorious Democratic candidate, James Buchanan, and the 8 secured by Whig candidate Fillmore. This was a clear sign of what was to come: the Whig Party was nearing its end, and the Republican Party was preparing to take its place, having emerged victorious in eleven of the fifteen Northern states.

The violent confrontations over slavery occurring in "Bleeding" Kansas were the most immediate problem that President Buchanan found himself facing, but, as many continued to fear for the stability of the Union, another event occurred, adding yet more fuel to the fire. The Supreme Court of the United States was called upon to examine the case of Dred Scott, a slave who had been freed north of the Missouri line and was claiming wage arrears. The Court ruled against Scott in 1857, on the grounds that the Missouri Compromise was unconstitutional, as Congress had no power to legislate over slavery in the territories, and had thus been void and ineffective from the beginning. The ruling greatly enraged the North (and the Free Soilers, in particular). The Union was already on a slippery slope, moving closer and closer toward the abyss, when, on October 16, 1859, a small group of armed men, led by "Captain" John Brown, raided and seized the federal armory at Harpers Ferry.

John Brown was an old abolitionist. He had fought in Bleeding Kansas, in which he had lost a son, and had been instrumental in several victories over the pro-slavery faction, as well as leading the Pottawatomie Massacre, in which five pro-slavery settlers were murdered. On a trip to Europe, he had become acquainted with romantic insurrectionism and had read, and been deeply influenced by, the treaty on partisan warfare by Piedmontese exile Carlo Bianco di Saint-Jorioz. By seizing Harpers Ferry, Brown aimed to incite a slave insurrection, take to the mountains with his band of rebels, and resist until this guerrilla warfare sparked a large-scale civil war, with the federal armies—urged on by popular pressure in the North—being forced to march on the South.

Brown's plan was entirely utopian and in a similar vein to the tragic expedition of Italian revolutionaries Carlo Pisacane and the Bandiera brothers. He was left isolated and, after a lengthy resistance, was forced to surrender. On December 2, he was found guilty and sentenced to death by hanging by a Virginia state court.

In such tense times, the incident had catastrophic consequences. Brown had shown courage during his detention and trial, eliciting respect and even admiration from his enemies. In his letters from prison, too, he proved extremely skillful in constructing his own legacy, omitting his plans to spark a bloody uprising and a catastrophic civil war and presenting himself, instead, as a faithful devotee to the cause of liberating slaves—an ideal for which he was now giving his life. These letters created a political storm in the North.

Brown became a hero and a martyr of freedom, and his memory was praised and celebrated all over, while Southerners were pilloried as torturers and wicked defenders of slavery.

Matters were even worse in the South. Public opinion now favored the notion that, without a shadow of a doubt, the North was preparing to unleash a revolt against the South—or, even worse, a civil war or massacre. A wave of terror swept over the region, as the Southern citizens—including those who condemned slavery—agreed that the time had come to lay such issues to rest and prepare for battle *pro aris et focis*.

The presidential elections of 1860 were approaching in this state of turmoil. The Democratic Party held its first convention in Charleston, South Carolina. The Democratic candidate, Senator Stephen Douglas of Illinois, was popular and well respected throughout the Union. With great political acumen, Douglas had realized that the Democratic Party was the only party to have preserved a national character and could thus appeal to potential voters in all states. The only trump card it had left to play, in a desperate attempt to preserve the Union, was the stable alliance between the South and the Midwest, the country's two large agricultural areas. However, for the alliance to hold strong, the Southerners would have to abandon all claims on the Western territories and leave them to the Free Soilers in the Midwest.

This would not have required—as careful analysis of the relevant historical documents confirms—the South to solemnly abandon its stance on slavery in the territories; it would have been enough for it to accept any sort of compromise postponing the *vexata quaestio*—an agreement, for example, along the lines of the Missouri Compromise or the Kansas-Nebraska Act. Although this would have done little to appease the more extremist Free Soilers (who were still a minority and had, for the most part, moved to the Republican Party), it would undoubtedly have ensured that the votes of the vast majority of Free Soilers in the Midwest went to Douglas and, therefore, the Democratic Party. Given that the Democrats could also rely on a strong Southern constituency, victory would have been virtually assured.

This would have been the rational way out of the crisis; rationality, however, had long since been swept away in a tide of emotion and partisanship (particularly in the South). The South felt it was facing the prospect of staying in the Union only as a tolerated minority, continually subjected to offence and abuse, and with a constant fear of aggression from the North. The Southern people felt that a compromise would be a taint, an admission of guilt; in the "family" that was the Union, they would be accepting the role of the degenerate younger brother, barely endured and scornfully lambasted.

Such fears were instrumental in the Southern delegates' decision, at the Charleston convention, to reject Douglas's proposal (which appeared anodyne to them) and demand that the electoral program of the Democratic Party include a clause explicitly guaranteeing and protecting the rights of slave owners in the territories. There was no way that the Midwesterners could accept this.

Leading figures remarked that, in making these demands, the Southern delegates were desperately defending a moot point, as there was no slavery in the territories—which, in themselves, were entirely unsuited to the agricultural, slave-based economy of the South, due to their climate and orographic and hydrographic characteristics. Slavery was nonexistent there, they argued, as were the conditions for it to develop. What these individuals failed to understand was that, for the South, slaveholding was not merely an abstract right but a very concrete matter of principle. History—as well as basic human experience—teaches us that compromise can often be reached in matters of a purely political nature (and that nearly all economic disputes can be resolved through compromise), but to compromise on matters of principle is a much more difficult, if not impossible, affair. Clashes of principle inevitably lead to a head-on collision—and, when entire populations are involved, straight to the battlefield.

In 1860, the situation had not yet reached this point, but the intransigence of the "Deep South" delegates on the clause protecting slavery (and, with it, their rejection of any sort of compromise that might discriminate against them or limit their rights as citizens) led them to abandon the Democratic Party. Indeed, while the Midwestern delegates nominated Senator Douglas as their presidential candidate, the Southerners formed their own convention and nominated Senator John C. Breckinridge of Kentucky, former vice president of the United States, Breckinridge was a moderate who defended both slavery and the Union and was a resolute defender of the South. Thus, the Democrats went to the elections with two candidates and—consequently—with the prospect of an almost certain defeat.

The Republican Party had, in the meantime, held its convention in Chicago and had nominated Abraham Lincoln for president. A lawyer from Illinois, Lincoln was a relative unknown, a dark horse for the election. It was precisely this quality (which meant he was not strongly disliked by anyone) that helped him prevail over the more well-known candidates, William H. Seward, Salmon P. Chase, and Edward Bates—all of whom, with their strong reputations, had hostile opposition within the convention. Lincoln was a native of Kentucky and thus had Southern origins, which further helped his cause; also, as the Illinois candidate, and a notorious Free Soiler to boot, he was the best equipped to oppose Douglas. Coming from a Whig background, Lincoln was essentially a conservative and would not have appeared threatening to the more moderate electorate.

Today, the literature on Abraham Lincoln is immense, yet on few other American statesmen are the ideas so confused. To clarify: Lincoln was not, and never had been, an abolitionist—if anything, the abolitionist movement viewed him with hostility. He was, without doubt, a resolute Free Soiler and, as such, was convinced that African American presence in America was a disaster. At length, he toyed with the idea of whether the problem might be resolved through mass deportation of the black population to Africa.

One thing was certain: despite being convinced that the federal government had no right to interfere with the institution of slavery where it already existed (i.e., the South), Lincoln was firmly opposed to slavery being introduced in the territories. This was not only driven only by his Free Soiler ideology but also by his future vision of the United States as a "great republic," a national state in the modern, nineteenth-century sense. Already at the time of his nomination, though no one had realized it yet, Lincoln aspired to become the great unifier of the American nation, similar to a Cavour or a Bismarck. Slavery evidently posed an obstacle to his plan, and—for this reason especially—it had to be confined to the South where it would eventually die out peacefully.

For Lincoln, slavery remained a secondary issue; the real problem was the Union's sovereignty over the territories, which, he believed, should be available for "free" labor and, on no accounts, accommodate the "peculiar institution." He adamantly rejected any talk of secession but maintained that a protective tariff was necessary to favor industrial development in the North. Lincoln had unrivalled political skill and farsightedness, combined with a deep sense of humanity—all qualities that contributed to making him one of the greatest statesmen of all time.

In the run-up to the election, matters had been complicated further when the Whigs, who felt they could not support the Democratic or Republican Party candidate, nominated Senator John Bell of Tennessee for president. This political faction, however, proved little more than a group of *laudatores temporis acti*, with no real electoral prospects.

Thus, with the Democratic Party split, and the Whig Party largely unpopular, when the presidential elections arrived, on November 6, 1860, Lincoln received 1,866,452 popular votes and 180 electoral votes, Breckinridge 849,781 popular votes and 72 electoral votes, and Bell 588,879 and 39 respectively. Ironically, Douglas received a good 1,376,957 popular votes but only 12 electoral votes. This was because he was the only truly national candidate (receiving votes from all over the Union), and his votes were thus so scattered around the country that he won only in Missouri and split New Jersey.

In any case, Abraham Lincoln's election as president of the United States was entirely correct and legitimate from a constitutional point of view (with his receiving 180 of 303 possible electoral votes). It did not matter that he received 1,866,452 popular votes against the 2,815,617 totaled by his three opponents: if we count the electoral votes, we can see that Lincoln would have won even if all the anti-Lincoln voters had united behind one of the other three candidates. Significantly, Lincoln had won without receiving a single electoral vote in the South, where he received very few popular votes—no more than 20,000 in the border states.

Shortly after Lincoln's victory, the South Carolina legislature called for elections to a special state convention, which assembled on December 17. Three days later, its delegates unanimously voted to secede from the Union. The die had been cast. On January 9, 1861, the state of Mississippi also seceded from the Union, followed by Florida on the 10th, Alabama on the 11th, Georgia on the 19th, Louisiana on the 26th, and Texas on February 1st. On February 4, 1861, representatives from the seven seceded states convened in Montgomery, Alabama. On February 7, the Montgomery Convention drafted the provisional constitution of the newly formed Confederate States of America. On the 9th, Senator Jefferson Davis of Mississippi was unanimously elected as provisional Confederate president.

Today, there is still a degree of uncertainty, among historians and otherwise, surrounding the figure of Davis—even more so than with Lincoln—and a truly satisfactory biographical study on him has yet to be written. Suffice it to say that Davis was a renowned figure, who had served as secretary of war under President Pierce and was a U.S. senator for the Democratic Party. He had acquired military experience in the war against Mexico, commanding a regiment of Mississippi volunteers, and had distinguished himself for bravery and been gravely wounded. Ultimately, however, he did not aspire to be president and would have preferred to have held a military post within the Confederacy.

This goes to show just how little concern Davis had for political careering, as he had never really considered himself a professional politician and had never been one. In line with the aristocratic mentality of the large-plantation owners of the South, he considered engagement in political activity as both a right and a duty, much like Roman senators in the Republican Age. It has rightly been pointed out that in the old, aristocratic South it was still customary to "work for politics," while in the modern, industrialized society that was developing in the North, a class of men was emerging who would rather "let politics work for them." As a political figure, Davis was free from the slightest trace of demagogy and never felt obliged to apologize or justify his actions, even in his most difficult hours—a trait that often led him to be accused of being haughty, standoffish, and stubborn. In point of fact, he served the South with the deepest dedication, unselfishly devoting his entire life to the cause, sacrificing his possessions and family, and performing his duty as he understood it, in spite of his physical frailty and poor health (among other things, he was almost blind in one eye).

At the time of his election, Davis was operating under no illusions: the North would not accept the secession without a reaction, even though the move was not illegal or prohibited by the Constitution. An immediate score to settle between the Confederacy and the Union came in the form of several federal forts that were manned by Unionist troops but located within Confederate boundaries. Among these, in particular, was Fort Sumter, a coastal fortification located in Charleston Harbor, South Carolina. Although President Lincoln had concluded his inaugural address with a plea for moderation, he had also made it clear that the Unionist troops would not abandon the fort.

What was to be done? Could the Confederacy tolerate "foreign" garrisons in its own backyard, completely undermining its newly proclaimed independence? When news broke out that the Union was preparing a military and naval expedition to bring supplies to Fort Sumter, the Confederacy felt obliged to act. General Beauregard, who was in command of Confederate troops in Charleston Harbor, received orders to demand Fort Sumter's surrender. When this was met with refusal, Southern batteries opened fire on the fort, forcing the Unionists—after a bombardment that caused no casualties—to haul down the flag and surrender. The date was April 13, 1861, and the Civil War had officially begun.

III

Lecture III

Before we look at the events of the Civil War, two questions bear consideration: (a) Why did the South resort to secession? (b) Why did the Confederate authorities take the initiative to order the bombardment of Fort Sumter?

The answer to the first question was initially considered very simple (and still is, by some historians): the South seceded from the Union in order to defend the "peculiar institution" of slavery. Even today, certain "politically correct" historians rehash this "explanation" in complete disregard of the fact that it has been totally discredited.

Indeed, no serious scholar can fail to see the absurdity of this reasoning. First and foremost, slavery *in the South* was not under threat from Lincoln, or the Republican Party, or the vast majority of Free Soilers. The Republican electoral program even promised a constitutional amendment to protect slavery indefinitely in those territories where it already traditionally existed, that is, the South. As such, safeguarding the institution of slavery would not have constituted a motive for the South's secession from the Union. Matters were different in the Western territories, where Lincoln and his party (as well as the Free Soilers, obviously) were determined not to let the "peculiar institution" take root. Let us not forget that for Lincoln these new territories were to remain an outlet for "free white people." The South, therefore, had to be categorically denied the right, however abstract a right it was, for its citizens to move there with their slaves. Southerners, consequently, found themselves facing a conflict of interests, which was to prove one of the most costly in history: when it came to migration to the territories, they would have to accept a limitation to their rights and, thus, theoretically become citizens of a lower rank.

In such a climate, it no longer mattered that a rational look at the geographical characteristics of the West was enough to reveal the unsuitability of an agricultural, slave-based economy there. This was certainly a reasonable objection to the South's intransigence; however, by that point, the matter had become so tempered by emotions and partisanship that it had become a point of principle. Any sort of compromise was deemed unacceptable.

All the same, the Southerners would have been in a far better position to defend their stance had they remained in the Union, which would have allowed them to argue their position in Congress (where, at least in the Senate, they could still have prevented any harmful measures being passed against them) and politically mobilize the part of the population (which was probably the majority) that seemed more inclined toward further compromise, rather than any excessively drastic measures. Ultimately, if defense of slavery really had been the South's sole concern (simply because its citizens were as "sinful," "wicked," and "unrepentant" as the more adamant abolitionists claimed), surely sufficient compensation could have been offered to make the slaveholders "see sense" and become "virtuous citizens." We must also bear in mind that the majority of Southerners were small farmers and landowners who did not actually own any slaves.

Thus, if not to defend slavery, what was the reason for secession? Essentially, the South was convinced (and not entirely wrongly) that, by staying in the Union, it would have been reduced to little more than a tolerated minority, with the constant fear that, sooner or later, the entire West would become a hotbed of violence, a large-scale Kansas of sorts. Additionally, the Southerners would have been forced to endure all those provisions favoring the North, such as the customs tariffs, which they found so oppressive and which would have effectively seen the South reduced to the status of a colony. On top of this, the North would have always been in a position to impose such provisions by using legislation regarding slavery as a means of blackmail.

As I have said before, the dispute with the North had become a matter of principle. Thus, the South decided to fend for itself, come what may—in the same way that a family member, who feels looked down on, mistreated, and tormented might leave home rather than endure such oppression any longer. Whether or not the South's fears would have ever materialized is another matter; the South *felt* threatened and acted accordingly. In the belief that their entire culture and civilization were at stake, the Southerners could find no other way to defend themselves than by pursuing the illusion of independence.

The matter of the bombardment of Fort Sumter presents some analogies. It is important to note that—contrary to what some historians maintain— Lincoln did not knowingly try to lure the Southerners into a trap by forcing them to fire the first shot. We must, however, realize that Lincoln thought there could be no solution to the secession crisis without the use of arms, and that if such a clash was to occur, it would be preferable that it take place sooner rather than later (as he wrote in a letter to a fellow politician). He also believed that, should this armed conflict occur, it was imperative that the government of the Union did not fire the first shot; whereas, if the South were to open hostilities, Lincoln would surely be able to count on the unified support of the entire North. Without the North behind him, he would not have been able to face a potential war with any hope of winning.

As for the Confederacy, from the very beginning, it had tried to negotiate the peaceful evacuation of the federally owned forts, receiving only categorical refusals from Union authorities. Under these tense conditions, the Confederate government felt that tolerating the Union's naval expedition to bring supplies to Fort Sumter would be a *capitis deminutio*, an acceptance of capitulation, and would undermine and ridicule the newly proclaimed independence. There is no doubt that the Confederates acted improvidently and were thus irrevocably caught up in the tide of events, but, in the given circumstances, it would have been morally difficult—if not impossible—to act otherwise.

As is often the case when armed conflict erupts, the American Civil War began in a fog of illusions. The most hardened Southerners regarded the North as a nation of shopkeepers, who did not know how to fight. They believed that a show of strength would be enough to bring the Union to the negotiating table. As for the Union government, it was convinced that secession had resulted from the scheming of a few meddling individuals and that the "good people" of the South would have willingly returned to the fold just as soon as these individuals had been dispersed or eliminated. Proof of this was Lincoln's belief that he could quash the "rebellion" with a militia of 70,000 volunteers, enlisted for three months—a paltry figure for a paltry length of time, all things considered.

The first serious consequence of this call to arms was that four other states seceded from the Union: Arkansas, Tennessee, North Carolina, and—most notably—Virginia, birthplace of George Washington and Thomas Jefferson, whose capital, Richmond, was chosen by the Confederate States to be the seat of their government.

The talk of war threw Washington into a frenzy. "To Richmond! To Richmond! Onward!" cried the newspapers. Thus, Lincoln's makeshift army set off, under the command of General Irvin McDowell, and hesitantly reached the Manassas Gap Railroad, on the river Bull Run, in Virginia. There, met by an equally makeshift Southern army under the command of Generals Beauregard and Johnston, they suffered a thorough defeat on July 21, 1861.

The Battle of Bull Run dispelled many of the initial illusions, and both sides began to prepare for outright war. The Union had already taken the first step by imposing a naval blockade on the Southern coasts. To avoid an international incident—and to recognize the legitimacy of the blockade itself—the great maritime powers of England and France had been forced to grant the Confederacy belligerent status, though not diplomatic recognition. Despite the North's absurd protests, the European powers had to recognize the Confederacy's existence—as for something to be blockaded it must evidently exist—which was necessary for the blockade to be recognized as legitimate action.

The South did not have a navy—it did not even have any ships—but the skillful and dynamic secretary of the navy, Stephen Russell Mallory, swiftly set to work countering the Union's naval threat by commissioning the construction of a limited number of very powerful ironclad warships, in addition to other state-of-the-art tools of war, such as electrically detonated limpet mines, assault crafts, and submarines. However, the South's decision to resort to technological warfare (perhaps the only strategic move that appeared possible) ultimately proved detrimental, as it was fighting an enemy who was far better equipped from an industrial point of view.

When the Union militia had completed its three-month term, the government of the Union issued a second call for volunteers for a period of three years, and shortly after, Congress granted the president permission to recruit up to 500,000 more volunteers. The Confederacy, however, was forced to adopt more drastic measures. The numerical inferiority of the South's white population (about five million against the eighteen million in the North) forced the Richmond government to introduce obligatory conscription, for the first time in the English-speaking world. Each side's organization did the rest, and a few months later, armies of hundreds of thousands were squaring up on battlefields throughout the country. By the end of the conflict, the Union would have mobilized around three million men, the Confederacy more than 1,400,000.

One aspect of the conflict that eluded almost everybody was just how radically and *qualitatively* different it would prove to be, in comparison to the Napoleonic wars, which still seemed fresh in the minds of the general public. This was because, between 1815 and 1861, the Industrial Revolution had explosively made its mark throughout the Western world. It affected the United States most of all and reinforced the major qualitative differences between North and South, which would eventually lead the South to secession and both sides to civil war.

Aside from introducing large-scale industry and, consequently, mass production in the North, the Industrial Revolution had brought with it a flurry of new inventions that forever changed the face of technology, and, concordantly, the very concept of warfare. The most remarkable thing was that the impact of so-called peacetime inventions on the outcome of the conflict was equivalent—and perhaps superior—to that of military innovations. The U.S. railway network, which by 1861 stretched 50,000 kilometers, enabled large quantities of troops, equipment, ammunition, and supplies to travel with a rapidity that would have been previously unimaginable; the electric telegraph (which covered more than 500,000 kilometers by 1861) made it possible to direct several military operations at the same time, on a number of often very distant fronts; the combine harvester led to an unprecedented increase in the speed and quantity of corn production, ensuring there was enough bread to feed entire armies, as well as the civilian population; and the invention of canned meat and condensed milk allowed soldiers to carry reserve supplies in a knapsack, thus reducing their burdensome reliance on fresh supplies and increasing autonomy and mobility. The sewing machine meant clothing could be rapidly mass-produced, and the vulcanization of rubber led to the mass manufacturing of cloaks, boots, and waterproof tents, allowing military operations to continue through the winter, whatever the climate.

If, on top of all this, we consider that bayonets had been rendered virtually obsolete by the rifled musket, able to hit a target over one thousand meters away (rather than the one hundred of the smoothbore rifle)—along with the prominent role played by the steamship and by rifled artillery-firing explosive and armor-piercing rounds—we realize that the North American people essentially fought the first industrial war in history, the first to be decided, in a sense, by the manufacturing capacity of the factories rather than the military genius of the commanders.

The Bull Run campaign had shown that, for the moment, the North's enormous strength—both military and industrial—was still largely a potential resource. The South, too, had military potential to develop, though its resources were much more limited. In such conditions, both sides spent the autumn and winter months of 1861–1862 mobilizing troops, organizing their respective campaigns, and training their militaries. By the time spring of 1862 came around, both sides had large, well-armed, and well-trained armies that were ready to fight. With his expectations of a short war shattered, President Lincoln's consequent strategy consisted in applying constant pressure on all fronts, in order to capitalize on the numerical and organizational superiority of the Union forces. Sooner or later, he believed, they would open a breach in enemy lines, through which the decisive charge could be led.

The Confederacy's strategy was simpler and predominantly dictated by its political aspirations, which were to gain independence rather than to bring down the Union. Its strategy was defensive through and through and based solidly on the hope that once the Union realized the Confederate armies could not be overpowered, it would be worn down by the conflict and agree to recognize Confederate independence. After all, "the defensive form of warfare" is, according to Prussian military theorist Carl von Clausewitz, "intrinsically stronger than the offensive"—though the Southern leaders did not take this fully into account. This defensive strategy partially made up for the Confederacy's significant limitations, in terms of soldiers and material means.

The fact of the matter was that the South had reached the era of industrial warfare with a remarkably backward economy. Agriculture in the South was still semicolonial in nature, consisting predominantly of large-scale monoculture crops, and entirely subject to the needs of the global, capitalist market. Cotton was the dominant crop—as were tobacco, sugar, and rice, to a lesser extent—and its overproduction had a detrimental effect on the farming of agricultural food products, which were essential for the sustenance of civilians and troops alike. Industrial equipment did exist in the South, but it was largely outdated and more suited to industries predating the Industrial Revolution, such as handicraft and artisanal trade. Despite being fairly extensive, the South's railroad network was also of a "preindustrial" nature, in that it was designed primarily to fulfill agricultural needs. Its lines were isolated and disconnected, with very few large lines crossing the entire South, as most were intended for short hauls, to transport cotton from the plantations to the sea. The lack of a specialized workforce (which was a predominant feature of the Northern economy) meant that, regardless of how outdated its factories were, industrial production in the South would have been comparatively slow in any case, occasionally even falling into a slump.

With an enormous strain to its economy, the Confederacy was forced to resort to extreme measures, building a network of arms-manufacturing industries essentially from scratch and placing its preexisting industry under military control. Although these measures would have been enough to allow the South to hold out resistance, it was still far from matching the North's industrial resources. The Civil War can thus be viewed as an industrial war, fought between two states: a modern, industrially advanced state and a backward, agricultural one, with the latter struggling desperately, aided by its dedication and strong leadership, to keep up with the former. In this sense, we may say that, from the outset, the South fought a rearguard fight in an attempt to delay the relentless march of the enemy as much as it could.

Despite its industrial superiority, victory for the North was far from being at hand. Although strong, its numerical superiority was anything but overwhelming and a long way off, at least initially, from the twofold superiority that Clausewitz believes is necessary to irrevocably counterbalance the skill of even the greatest commanders and guarantee victory. This occurred for a number of reasons. First and foremost, as mentioned above, with the widespread perception of the North as an oppressive and threatening presence, an enemy at the gates, the South was able to introduce conscription almost straight away, while the North could not. Too many people in the North believed that if the Southern states truly wanted to leave the Union, no law or moral power could be invoked to forcefully keep them in it. Thus, the proposal of introducing conscription in the North was met with almost universal hostility. War, it was widely believed, should be fought by volunteers—namely, those who believed it was a necessity and subscribed to its objectives—and although many volunteers signed up—enticed by enlistment rewards and a three-year term limit—there were not enough of them to guarantee the North overwhelming superiority over the South. When, after much tergiversation, the North also decided to pass a draft law, the Enrollment Act of 1863, a riot broke out among the working classes in New York, and, after several days of violence in the streets, the military had to be called in to suppress the mob and restore order.

Another serious obstacle that the Northern strategists found themselves facing was the sheer vastness of the enemy territory that they had to invade, conquer, and subdue. The Confederacy was five times bigger than France and twice the size of France, Italy, England, and Germany put together. The task of mastering such an expansive territory, defended by men determined to fight to the death, would have made any military leader tremble.

No long-term military operations had been planned, as they had been deemed unnecessary amid the initial hopes for a short war. General plans of action were drawn up only after the Union's defeat at Bull Run had proved to both sides that the war would be a long and bloody one.

The theater of operations was divided roughly in two by the Allegheny Mountain Range, which runs roughly parallel to the Atlantic coast and increasingly inland as it progresses southward. In Virginia, the distance between the mountains and the ocean is less than one hundred kilometers, creating a bottleneck that offers an advantage to the defender, while in Georgia, this distance rises to five hundred kilometers. At the time of the Civil War, the Allegheny Mountains constituted a formidable obstacle: they were vast and covered by impenetrable forests, almost entirely devoid of roads (the few that existed were little more than muddy trails and thus useless in rainy conditions), and virtually unpopulated and lacking in food supplies for both men and animals.

Between the ocean and the mountain range, and with the protection of the latter, sit the four states that made up, so to speak, the heart of the Confederacy: Virginia, North and South Carolina, and Georgia—among the most densely populated and wealthy states of the Southern nation.

Beyond the Alleghenies lies a vast, undulating plateau, which increasingly grades down until it reaches a big river and levels out. The northern part of the Allegheny Plateau is crossed by two major rivers, the Tennessee and Cumberland Rivers, which flow in a northwesterly direction into the Ohio River, not far from where it meets the Mississippi River. Progressing westward, the terrain between these two rivers becomes gradually less hilly, and it is this stretch of land that was to be another theater of operations, where Northern forces would attempt a large-scale flanking maneuver, circumnavigating the Alleghenies from the South and opening a gap at Chattanooga, through which to penetrate into Georgia.

Control of the Mississippi River valley was also of vital importance for both sides. Many of the Confederacy's most important cities could be found there—from Memphis, Tennessee, to New Orleans, Louisiana, the largest urban center in the South, while, for the North, control of the immense river not only would have meant cutting the Confederacy in two, restricting its supplies from the West, but also would have acted as an excellent base for the Union armies to support the great flanking maneuver mentioned above.

Finally came the West—dominated, in the new Confederacy, by the huge state of Texas. The almost complete absence of roads and railways in the West made large-scale operations impossible there; nevertheless, the West was of monumental importance to the Confederates for its precious supplies of beef, horses for the cavalry and artillery, and mules for haulage. It also served as a major thoroughfare to Mexico, which, in times of naval blockade, was vital for purposes of trade.

From the onset of the conflict, it was immediately clear that one of the Union's foremost objectives was to cut the West off from the rest of the Confederacy. Unfortunately for the South, its strategic reaction to this was inadequate and fundamentally flawed, as it accepted the Mississippi River line as the division between two sectors, disregarding the fundamental principle that such a separation line should never coincide with an area that is particularly vulnerable to enemy penetration. As the war progressed, the consequences of this strategic shortsightedness would become evident.

In the North, the first to clearly draw up a strategic military plan to bring down the Confederacy was the aging general Winfield Scott. At the time, Scott, a native of Virginia who had stayed faithful to the Union, held the post of general in chief of the United States. Despite being old and tormented by gout pains by the time war erupted, Scott was still clear thinking and astute. The plan he laid out to the Union authorities envisaged the creation of a large fleet of ironclad river gunboats, which would escort a powerful convoy of troops; advancing rapidly with a central thrust down the Mississippi, the Union would thus seize the river and cut off the Confederate states west of it, while, to the east, the naval blockade would choke the Confederacy's economy and supply lines.

Unsurprisingly, Scott's plan was met with criticism from the armchair strategists. They scoffed at the slowness of the maneuver (which would have lead to a slow strangulation of the Confederacy, rather than the lightening annihilation that many hoped for), and the press mockingly named it the Anaconda Plan, after the giant Amazonian snake that slowly strangles its prey in its coils.

Those were, of course, the heated times of the "To Richmond! To Richmond! Onward!" sloganeering—the bellicose mentality that had led to the Bull Run defeat. Naturally, Scott's plan was still only a draft and had a number of flaws—namely, that an expeditionary force of merely 40,000 men would be enough to seize the Mississippi River and that the blockade itself would be enough to secure victory, with no need for a pitched confrontation with the enemy. However, the Anaconda Plan also contained some excellent and insightful ideas. The first was that control of the Mississippi would be an essential step toward securing victory. The second (which Scott immediately put into practice) was that the Union should take advantage of the South's naval weakness and lack of preparation to seize the Mississippi from the Confederacy by capitalizing on its own industrial superiority and immediately launching a fleet of armored gunboats. The third—which came almost a century ahead of its time—was that the army and navy should operate in conjunction with one another.

Nevertheless, after the failure of the Bull Run campaign, President Lincoln summoned General George Brinton McClellan, who had been an official observer of the European armies in the Crimean War in 1855. McClellan quickly showed a distinct talent for organization and management. It was thanks to him that the masses of volunteers who had enlisted were raised into a 120,000-strong, well-trained army, with more than 500 cannons. This was the Army of the Potomac, destined to operate on the Virginian front. For all McClellan's achievements, he never fully understood just how important the Western front and the Mississippi were to the North's campaign, and this caused friction with Scott. The former believed the war was to be fought and decided in Virginia—at most, the other fronts were to act as decoys, to draw in enemy forces.

Thus, McClellan set about preparing the campaign of 1862, first insisting that Scott be removed from the post of general in chief and that he be appointed in his place. Under this new leadership, the West became of secondary importance—another tactical shortcoming that would prove influential.

As mentioned above, at this time, the South had no general plan of action other than to remain on the defensive on all fronts. However, this strategy—which was in line with its political agenda of defending secession, rather than attacking the Union—had a fundamental flaw, in that it left any strategic initiative entirely in the enemy's hands.

It is also important to note that the South did not have a general in chief until almost the end of the war. Confederate President Jefferson Davis was not without military experience: for many years, he had served as U.S. secretary of war and had commanded a regiment of volunteers from his native Mississippi in the Mexican-American War, emerging as a hero from the battle of Buena Vista, in which he had been seriously wounded. At the outbreak of the Civil War, he would have preferred to have held a high military post within the Confederacy; as such, once he was elected to the presidency, he invoked the constitutional clause stating that in the Confederacy, as in the Union, the president had supreme command and direction of the armed forces. Strategic directives would, therefore, have to be issued by the head of state; however, given the many duties that the presidential office entailed, this would have to be delegated to a military adviser, in this case, a general who was in charge of the South's military under the direct supervision of the president. This was the worst solution to the problem of military leadership that could have been implemented. The military adviser had no effective powers, but direction of the operations nonetheless rested entirely on his shoulders, as the president was overwhelmed by the multitude of state affairs. He thus carried the burden of his decisions, but could enjoy none of the glory.

The situation was the same in the Confederate navy. President Davis, who was nominally commander in chief, left all powers to Stephen Mallory, secretary of the navy, a decision dictated by the great—and thoroughly deserved—confidence that the president had in him. Along with all the usual organizational tasks, Mallory thus had to take on the strategic direction of the navy and all naval operations as well. Throughout the war, neither the South nor the North ever had an admiralty or a chief of staff.

In the Union navy, thanks to Lincoln's political nous, the secretary of the navy, Gideon Welles—a level-headed man of common sense but little skill—was flanked by Assistant Secretary Gustavus Vasa Fox. Fox was a former naval officer and merchant captain, as well as a man of genius and exceptional intelligence, and for much of the war, he effectively performed the duties of a modern chief of naval operations.

As these political machinations occurred, both sides continued to mobilize their industrial apparatuses (vast in the North, meager in the South) and their scientists. The Civil War was one of the first conflicts to utilize scientists for military purposes, after the initial attempts made in revolutionary France. In the South, for example, the great oceanographer Matthew Fontaine Maury developed the electronically detonated naval mine, while, in the North, Joseph Henry, Alexander Dallas Bache, and, above all, John Ericsson lent their talents to the war effort, with the latter designing the ironclad gunboat USS *Monitor*.

The North's huge industrial apparatus set to work mass-producing war materials. By June 1892 (less than a year into the conflict), the factories had churned out 3,132 cannons, 1,297,411 artillery shells, 109,810 rifles, and 28,213,700 cartridges. By the end of the conflict, more than a billion cartridges and 3,371,878 cannons had been produced. These were—and still are—startling figures, even without considering the naval shipbuilding programs, which included the construction of a fleet of ironclad warships for the Western rivers.

The South was incapable of competing with such figures, but they confronted the challenge with a desperate energy of sorts. A massive Confederate Powder Works was built in Augusta, Georgia, and the few factories that existed were pushed to their limits; the blockade was also repeatedly violated so that huge quantities of arms could be imported from Europe.

The vast majority of blockade violators were British, and investors in Britain began setting up blockade-running businesses specializing in trade that was in violation of the blockade. These businesses engineered special ships that, compared to the usual merchant ships, were lower to the water, considerably faster, and burned high-grade anthracite coal, which gave off light-grey smoke, instead of telltale black. This activity proved very profitable, as supplies and firearms were badly needed, and it was calculated that if one blockade runner was captured or lost, after just eight trips, a profit of 700 percent would nonetheless be returned. Goods destined for the South generally left Europe on normal merchant ships heading to the Bahamas or Bermuda; there, they were transferred aboard the blockade runners, which, in one night and with a little luck, could reach the Southern ports of Wilmington, Charleston, Savannah, or Mobile.

It was thanks to these blockade runners that the Confederacy managed to import 600,000 rifles and 680,000 kilograms of lead over the course of the war. By September 1863 (roughly two years into the conflict), the South had produced or imported 150,000 small arms, 677 cannons, 298,305 artillery shells, and 44,933,907 cartridges. These are paltry figures in comparison to the numbers in the North, but they nonetheless provided the Confederacy with a basic supply of armaments with which to put up a fight.

The real problems the Confederacy found itself facing were in other areas. First of all, the blockade runners worked solely for profit, rather than out of any sort of devotion to the Southern cause. For this reason, they were often reluctant to transport arms and munitions, as these constituted heavy and bulky loads with low profitability per kilogram and, above all, were considered dangerous cargo. Indeed, one well-placed grenade from a Northern cruiser would be enough to blow up any blockade runner carrying explosives. Blockade runners thus sought to prioritize high-value, low-risk goods in small amounts, such as French perfumes, bottles of champagne, and fine wine, silks, fashionable clothing, and ostrich feathers. It was virtually impossible to find any of these products in the South, and they were consequently worth their weight in gold (or cotton, as the blockade runners were paid in cotton, which they later resold in Europe at four times the price).

This trade of luxuries posed a serious problem for the Confederacy, and extreme measures were adopted to fight it, the most of extreme of which being the complete nationalization of trade under Jefferson Davis's government. From that moment onward, there was an extraordinary growth in the influx of arms and ammunition, while luxury goods petered out almost entirely.

The South's other major setback had to do with its railways. Before the war, locomotives, wagons, and rail lines had been produced almost entirely in the North—a source that had naturally been cut off when the hostilities had begun. To make matters worse, the South had been forced to abandon its limited production of railroad equipment, as all its industrial resources were devoted to the production of armaments. Lacking in construction and repair, the Southern railways began deteriorating fast. The tracks were the first to give way, followed by the rolling stock. Accidents were becoming increasingly frequent; indeed, one Confederate soldier pointed out that traveling by train from Atlanta to Richmond had become more dangerous than patrolling the front line. This had tragic consequences for the Southern population. Firstly, transport of goods for civilian use was almost entirely suppressed. Secondly, the transport of military supplies was given absolute priority over anything else, and this led to goods being poorly distributed so that in Georgia, for example, food supplies were plentiful, while in Virginia, people were on the verge of starvation. This situation was made even worse by the common practice of melting down railroad iron and using it to plate warships.

On top of all of this, much of the railroad personnel came from the North or was sympathetic to the Northern cause. It is still difficult to quantify the degree of sabotage that went on, but it certainly did occur and with serious consequences. On the Virginian front, for example, General Lee lamented the poor functioning of the Richmond, Fredericksburg, and Potomac Railroad, which was vital for supplies. Modern historians have discovered that the superintendent of the railroad, Samuel Ruth, was in fact a Union spy, which explains a great deal of its shoddy functioning.

The full effects of the collapse of the Confederate rail network have yet to be quantified (and should be done so urgently); however, it was certainly this collapse—and not the Northern blockade—that caused the lack of food and forage supplies on the front lines, especially during the terrible winter of 1864–1865.

But as the year 1861 drew to a close, these problems were still far away. The North and (to a lesser extent) the South still clung to the illusion of a short war. Aware of the great strength of their forces, the Unionists, in particular, believed that the campaign of 1862 would be decisive.

IV

Lecture IV

In 1862, the Civil War began in earnest and assumed dimensions that few had foreseen at the outset, as it rapidly became a conflict of gigantic proportions, an inconceivable tragedy, and the first *total* war of the industrial era. By the early months of that year, the two huge armies were squaring up for direct confrontation, with the North still nursing the illusion that it could use its military strength to crush the South in a single, magnificent campaign.

According to McClellan, the outcome of this campaign would be decided in Virginia, with the other fronts playing only a secondary, almost negligible role of carrying some of the military burden. For this reason, from an early stage in the conflict, the general in chief of the Union had begun to make insistent requests for further reinforcements to counter the "superiority of the enemy." He wanted these reinforcements to be taken from the Western fronts, which he considered much less important.

President Lincoln, however, was not in agreement on this matter, nor was the Union navy. From the onset of the conflict, the secretary of the navy, Gideon Wells, had appointed a Blockade Strategy Board, also known as the Commission of Conference, made up of eminent scientific and military personalities, and the latter had been quick to point out that the Paris Declaration of 1856, signed by the leading European powers, posed a number of problems to the implementation of the blockade. For the blockade to be recognized by neutral states, it was no longer enough for it to be proclaimed on paper and enforced only when and where it seemed opportune—the blockade had to be formally proclaimed, promptly established, and enforced by a cordon of ships assigned the specific task of capturing or intercepting any vessels attempting to reach the blockaded coasts.

We may legitimately suspect that the signatories of the Paris Declaration had intended to make the blockade impossible: after all, how could warships be expected to station in front of coasts as dangerous as those of the Atlantic, especially in the winter seasons, braving the notoriously violent storms that had led the waters of Cape Hatteras to become known as "the graveyard of the Atlantic"?

Nevertheless, the men of the Blockade Strategy Board and the leaders of the Union navy (including, in particular, the brilliant Gustavus Vasa Fox) had no intention of giving up on the blockade. To meet the conditions of the declaration, they planned a series of landing operations to capture a number of key Southern ports that they intended to use as Union bases of operations—thus granting the navy constant access to the sea to enforce the blockade. The first of these operations was conducted on August 27, 1861, when a naval squadron under the command of Flag Officer Silas Stringham stormed the Hatteras Inlet. A devastating naval bombardment forced Forts Hatteras and Clark to surrender, and the Union troops—who had slogged ashore—gained a foothold on the North Carolina coast. On November 7, a similar operation, this time led by Flag Officer Samuel F. DuPont, had captured Forts Walker and Beauregard and the towns of Beaufort and Port Royal, South Carolina.

These operations, initially intended for the sole purpose of enforcing the blockade, had alerted the Union navy leaders to the entirely new possibility of employing maritime forces as a genuine means of invasion, rather than simply to control naval routes. This enabled amphibious assault to be launched on a previously unheard of scale, opening new fronts on the Confederate coastline and inaugurating a new type of warfare that, honed to perfection in subsequent years, would become distinctive of the U.S. armed forces and be employed successfully in several conflicts.

With this newfound awareness of the navy's capacity for assault, the Union leaders and President Lincoln proposed a similar operation but on a much larger scale: to seize the Mississippi River and capture the great city of New Orleans. When McClellan was consulted, he gave his consent; after all, the operation would require only a fairly limited number of land forces and would divert Confederate attention from the huge offensive surge he was preparing in Virginia. In spite of this, on March 11, 1862, Lincoln removed McClellan as general in chief, leaving him in charge only of the Army of the Potomac and making him pay the price for underestimating the value of the other fronts.

However, even before McClellan could make his move, two other events had substantially altered the strategic framework of the conflict. The first of these happened in the West, where the Confederate forces, under the command of General Albert Sidney Johnston, had formed a long line to defend the southern regions of Kentucky and Tennessee. Due to its imposing length, the line was very vulnerable, as it was inadequately manned by forces spread too thinly along it. Johnston had committed the error of attempting an all-too-comprehensive defense, and the risk was that it would be unable to contain the enemy. Two rivers, the Cumberland and Tennessee, ran perpendicular to this defensive deployment. As these rivers were vulnerable to potential enemy penetration, the Confederates had built Fort Henry on the Tennessee River and Fort Donelson on the Cumberland to protect the passage and defend Tennessee and the South from invasion.

A little-known Unionist general, one Ulysses Simpson Grant, had fully gauged the strategic significance of these two rivers and the enormous military and naval advantage that control of the waters, achievable with the Union's powerful flotilla of ironclad gunboats, would bring. Grant also recognized the importance of cooperating effectively with the navy, a strategic focus that would feature significantly in his subsequent military initiatives.

Once he had obtained the permission of General Henry Halleck, commander of the Western theater, Grant moved against Fort Henry on February 2, 1862, in close collaboration with the ironclad gunships of the Union navy under Flag Officer Andrew H. Foote. At one time a soldier himself, Grant would go on to become one of the Union's most brilliant strategists and one of the greatest military leaders of all time. His firm belief in joint army-navy operations provided a model for future operations and differentiated him from McClellan, who never truly understood, or saw the need for, joint expeditions, as he conceived of the navy solely as a means of troop transportation.

Fort Henry fell on February 6, 1862, under a barrage of gunfire from the naval units. After the surrender, Grant wasted no time and immediately pushed on toward Fort Donelson, which, however, posed a far tougher challenge. After successfully staving off the assault of the Union gunboats, the Confederate forces garrisoned inside Fort Donelson launched a surprise attack that came close to forcing the besieging army to retreat. On February 16, however, the fort garrison finally capitulated under Unionist pressure, accepting Grant's terms of "unconditional surrender" and handing over 14,623 prisoners, 2 generals, and 62 cannons. On February 25, Union forces occupied Nashville, the capital of Tennessee.

These victories had shown that the Western fronts could be decisive and highlighted their enormous strategic importance, which had been greatly underestimated by McClellan. They did not, however, lead the general to change his views or alter his plans, until something happened in Virginia that significantly hindered them.

The naval strategy of the Confederate secretary of the navy, Stephen Russell Mallory, was finally taking shape in Virginia. Focusing more on quality than quantity, it hinged on countering the enemy's overwhelming naval superiority with a technological innovation that it was not expecting: the ironclad warship. With painstaking efforts, Confederate industry—which was in a sorry state compared to the North's—had managed to produce the first ironclad warship, converting and armoring the remains of the steam frigate USS *Merrimack*. The ship was renamed the *Virginia* and was in action by March 8, 1862, upsetting all of McClellan's plans.

The Union general had in fact been planning on organizing the transportation of the entire Army of the Potomac by water, on several imposing convoys, to Urbanna, on the east coast of Virginia. Landing there, he believed, would allow his troops to outflank Confederate General Joseph E. Johnston's forces in northern Virginia and capture the Confederate capital of Richmond almost by surprise.

McClellan's plan warrants careful consideration, in particular the merit of its goal. Possession of Richmond was undoubtedly of vital importance for the Confederacy. The city was home to the renowned Tredegar Iron Works, the most important foundry in the South and the only one that could compete even remotely with the industrial giants in the North. Holding onto Richmond was also critical, as, aside from its industrial output, the Confederate capital was a real symbol of the South, and to lose it would have certainly inflicted a morale-crushing blow.

Nevertheless, the Confederacy did possess other industrial centers, which they were developing with untiring energy, and, as far as Richmond's symbolic value was concerned, the capital could simply be moved to wherever the Confederate congress and president sat. Thus, losing Richmond would certainly have been a major setback but probably not a fatal one; much more instrumental to Confederate resistance was General Joseph Johnston's army, and that would be left untouched and ready to attack McClellan's troops.

For McClellan's plan to succeed, it was essential that Unionist troops retain control of the James River, a vital line of operation running through Richmond, which led straight to the political and military center of Confederate power. To sustain an army of over 120,000 men, with hundreds of guns and thousands of quadrupeds, would have been impossible without a line of operation able to guarantee a continuous flow of thousands of tons of supplies, ammunition, food, reinforcements, and other materials of a varied nature. The James River was this line, and it cut to the heart of the Confederacy like a knife.

The river, which flows into the harbor area of Hampton Roads, Virginia, was kept under firm Union control by shore batteries stationed at its mouth, which were supported by two old but powerful ships—the corvette *Cumberland* and the frigate *Congress*, both heavily armed. However, on March 8, 1862, the ironclad *Virginia* launched an unexpected attack, making light work of the shore batteries and sinking both the *Cumberland* and *Congress*. The James was once again under Confederate control, barring the way for McClellan and his plans.

The Army of the Potomac had been deprived of its best line of operation, and its movements were heavily delayed as a result. The York River was adopted in place of the James but proved much less effective. The general slowdown affected the overall progress of the campaign and granted General Joseph Johnston's Confederate infantry enough time to reach Richmond and organize a defensive deployment. The *Virginia*, in the meantime, had become queen of the waters. Although the Union navy had produced a similar warship, the *Monitor*, it had been unable to destroy the Southern "monster."

All these events radically altered McClellan's strategic outlook and exposed the true nature of the war—now undeniably a global conflict on all fronts, which could not be resolved in a single theater of operations as he had thought. Any remaining illusions about the duration of the war were at this point shattered.

Indeed, far from acting as little more than a diversion, Union forces in the West were in full offensive action. The Federal forces there had been organized into two armies: the Tennessee Army, led by General Ulysses Grant, and the Cumberland Army, under the command of Don Carlos Buell. On April 6, 1862, the Confederate Army of Tennessee, led by General Albert Sidney Johnston, attacked Grant at Pittsburg Landing, in the hope of crushing him before the anticipated arrival of Buell's men as reinforcements. The attempt failed. After initial success, the Confederate troops were repulsed, and Johnston was wounded and died. The new Southern commander, General Beauregard, had to order retreat, allowing Grant and his men to advance into northern Mississippi. Worse was yet to come for the Southerners. On April 24, Flag Officer David Glasgow Farragut ran his fleet of Union warships past Forts Jackson and St. Philip, which defended New Orleans, capturing the city and leaving the entire course of the Mississippi River open for the taking.

Although McClellan had still not made his move, the situation for the Confederates had suddenly become very serious after the catastrophic events on the Western fronts. Confederate leaders in Richmond knew that the Army of the Potomac, with its more than 112,000 men, posed another terrible threat that, in some way, had to be forestalled.

On April 13, President Davis summoned General Robert Edward Lee to Richmond and entrusted him with the direction of military operations, under presidential control. The task seemed an impossible one, but Lee devoted himself to it with extreme commitment.

A native of Virginia, Lee was opposed to secession and slavery but had answered the call to arms by lending his military experience and skills to the Confederate cause. Highly regarded by Federal General Winfield Scott (who had wanted him in charge of the Unionist armies), Lee was still relatively unknown in the South, though he would go on to accrue immense fame and become a symbol of the South itself, idolized by his soldiers and feared by his enemies.

Nowadays, criticism of Lee has, to some degree, become fashionable, with historians pointing out that, although he was hostile to slavery, he had been a slave owner and served the "pro-slavery" South. He was also an old-fashioned general, who never understood the full potential of new weaponry, preferring such antiquated methods as the bayonet charge, and he failed to comprehend that, in modern warfare, defense prevailed over attack. He concentrated too much of his efforts on the Virginian front and often neglected other theaters of operation. He was tormented by deep personal crises—and the list could go on.

Many of these observations are undoubtedly true. However, together, they make up a fragmentary, Jesuitical truth of a dogmatically intransigent nature. Such criticism does not take into account (or deliberately chooses to ignore) the overall picture, the complete panorama, with its light and shade and historical perspective. What, then, is our historical appraisal of the man who, more than any other, helped keep the Confederacy afloat for four years?

No historian or scholar who has remained impartial and has resisted being misled by political correctness can, in good faith, deny Lee's greatness as a military leader. As such, he takes his place in history alongside such commanders as Epaminondas, Hannibal, or Napoleon. Lee was similar to Epaminondas in his strategic vision, and it is a complete fallacy that his view of the conflict was restricted to the Virginian front (we only have to look to his voluminous correspondence to make sure of that). Like Hannibal—and perhaps more than any other leader—Lee knew the "art" of war, and just like Napoleon, he was a master of using timing to his advantage, operating with lightning attacks.

Lee was immensely popular with his soldiers and had succeeded in forging a supremely effective military unit, the Army of Northern Virginia, which was mobile and flexible, compact as steel, and well worthy to stand alongside the most famous armies in history. This army alone is enough to prove Lee's merit. Contrary to common belief, generals are not usually particularly popular with their soldiers, but Lee's men often begged him to not expose himself in conflict, as they were ready to die for him but not run the risk of losing him. Indeed, the admiration and respect that Lee's troops had for him are the true mark of his greatness.

Lee was also one of the most competent strategists of all time. On several occasions, he successfully pulled off what Count Helmuth von Moltke describes as the most difficult operation in war: the simultaneous bringing together of two separate armies on the same battlefield, at the right time. He had a very sharp eye for the terrain and used timing to a devastating effect.

We must now consider his negative aspects, which no man lacks. Lee's shortcomings are rooted in the very structure of the society that produced him and that he fought to defend. The civilization of the Old South certainly had its charms, but history had left it behind. It was condemned to die out, and the last chance it had was to die standing. It was a society of the past that looked to the past and lived in the past. Lee was never (nor could he have been) a general of the new industrial age, such as Grant, and this is where his genius lay. The best way to define Lee is as the last general of the Napoleonic age and, as such, one of the greats.

Once Lee had accepted his post as military adviser to President Davis, his most pressing concern was the situation in Virginia, where the situation continued to get worse. Aware that his troops would be unable to defend everything, General Joseph Johnston had reluctantly decided to sacrifice the naval base at Norfolk in order to consolidate defense of Richmond. Unfortunately for the Confederates, this evacuation meant that the *Virginia* had no home port and nowhere to go and had to be destroyed to be kept from enemy hands.

But what Lee had in mind for Virginia was an artful use of strategic intimidation, which would start from the Shenandoah valley. From early on in the war, the valley had acted as headquarters to General Thomas Jonathan Jackson, whose firm resistance at Bull Run had earned him the nickname "Stonewall." Jackson, a devout Bible reader, was a clever, bold, and resourceful leader. Lee urged Jackson to attack the Union forces threatening the valley, forcing them back and feigning a threat to Washington, the Federal capital. Jackson's offensive meant that the army corps of General McDowell (which was on its way to reinforce McClellan's) had to be held back to defend the capital. McClellan was thus left isolated, and on May 31, Lee cast General Johnston and his men against him. The Battle of Seven Pines ensued but ended inconclusively. However, General Johnston had been wounded in action and was forced to give up command to Lee, who took his place at the head of what he would christen the Army of Northern Virginia. This was to be a historic moment.

Lee resumed his plans, ordering Jackson to join up with his army, on forced march and in secret, from the Shenandoah valley, where he had defeated all his adversaries, and on June 26, 1862, Lee's roughly 97,000 men attacked McClellan's 105,000. The Seven Days Battles followed in the form of a series of violent and bloody confrontations, which resulted in the retreat of McClellan's men—who had come to within four kilometers of the Confederate capital—toward the safety of Harrison's Landing on the James River. The threat to Richmond had been thwarted, but at Malvern Hill, Lee had revealed his greatest weakness: his failure to understand the new power of rifled weapons and his faith in Napoleonic-style bayonet charges. These shortcomings had led his forces to incur serious and avoidable losses, without any local victories.

In the West, however, the situation remained serious. General Halleck, in charge of that particular front, had been forced to make the difficult decision to move his two armies in diverging lines, corresponding (as I mentioned above) to the lines of operation of the Western theater. General Buell led his men on a leisurely march southeast, toward Chattanooga, while General Grant, with the support of the Union's ironclad gunboats, headed for the final Confederate bulwark on the Mississippi, the stronghold of Vicksburg.

After capturing New Orleans, Flag Officer Farragut had sailed up the great Mississippi with his fleet, and Vicksburg found itself under attack from two large Unionist fleets, from north and south. On land, too, General Grant's forces bore down on the defensive lines surrounding the well-fortified city.

Before New Orleans had fallen into enemy hands, the Confederate navy had begun constructing four ironclad warships on the Mississippi. Three of these warships had not been completed in time, but the Confederates had managed to save one, the *Arkansas*, from destruction. In the hands of skillful and energetic Captain Isaac N. Brown, work on the warship had been completed in record time, and on July 15, 1862, the *Arkansas* launched a solitary attack on the two enemy fleets combined. It was an epic battle, with the *Arkansas* once again showing that the future belonged to warships. Even though the warship eventually had to be destroyed due to serious engine problems, it had served its purpose; with Farragut retreating to New Orleans, the Confederates regained control of some three hundred kilometers of the Mississippi—defended on either end by the strongholds of Vicksburg and Port Hudson—and the Confederacy was saved from being cut in two. Thus, the Unionist threat was momentarily thwarted in the West.

But the situation in Virginia was still serious. Lincoln had called General Henry Halleck back from the Western theater, assigning him the post of general in chief, and had formed a major new unit, the Army of Virginia, and appointed General John Pope as its commander. Pope's army had left the Washington area to march on Richmond along the traditional land route (and was thus separated from McClellan's men), and Lee saw the opportunity to strike. He left a veil of troops to watch over McClellan (who had not shown the slightest sign of wanting to attack) and launched a forced march against Pope.

When Lee's forces reached the enemy, he showed no hesitation in dividing them. He sent his II Army Corps, led by Stonewall Jackson, to perform a wide-ranging flanking maneuver, attacking the enemy's flank and rearguard, while his I Corps (under the command of General Longstreet) attacked frontally. On August 29, 1862, on the fields of Manassas—in what was to be known as the Second Battle of Bull Run—Pope was soundly defeated and forced to retreat north of the Potomac River.

Thus, by the end of August 1862, all threats to the Confederacy had been neutralized. The ball, so to speak, was now in their court, and they began to believe that perhaps the conflict could be resolved in a single campaign, if they were to go on the offensive. In early September, Lee invaded Maryland;

in the West, the Army of Tennessee—newly led by General Braxton Bragg, who had replaced General Beauregard—penetrated into Kentucky, and, further west, General Van Dorn attacked Grant on the border between Mississippi and Tennessee.

Meanwhile, Lincoln had hastily recalled McClellan and his Army of the Potomac (which had absorbed units from General Pope's disbanded Army of Virginia), and at Antietam, in Maryland, they confronted Lee's army on September 16 and 17. The battle was one of the bloodiest in the war and ended in a stalemate, with Lee having to withdraw to Virginia. At least on that front, the Southern offensive was over.

In Kentucky, the Confederate offensive continued. General Bragg had managed to occupy the state capital, Frankfort, and install a Confederate governor, but success proved fleeting. On October 5, Van Dorn was defeated by Grant at Corinth, and on October 8, Bragg attacked Perryville unsuccessfully and was forced to retreat from Kentucky into East Tennessee. The Confederate offensive, much like the Unionist one before it, had failed on all fronts.

There was yet to be a final flare-up in the campaign of 1862. In Virginia, McClellan was made to pay the price for his indecisiveness, and Lincoln appointed General Ambrose Burnside to replace him at the head of the Army of the Potomac. The new commander advanced quickly toward the Rappahannock River, a major obstacle on the route to Richmond, in order to steal a march on Lee and surprise him by crossing the river at Fredericksburg. Lee, however, was not one to fall for such traps, and when Burnside reached the north bank of the river, he found the Confederate divisions already lined up and waiting on the other side. He decided to attempt to force the passage all the same. The battle of Fredericksburg thus took place on December 13, and the Union suffered a bloody defeat.

Later that month, on December 29, in the Western theater, one of Grant's corps commanders, Union General William T. Sherman, attempted to capture Vicksburg by land attack, only to be thwarted with heavy casualties in the Battle of Chickasaw Bayou.

The campaign of 1862 had involved large armies, and both sides had suffered immense and unprecedented losses. After such devastation, both sides were forced to relinquish their initial optimistic expectations of a swift, clean victory.

Technological innovations allowed conflict to continue throughout the winter months, and operations raged on. The year 1863 had barely begun when at Murfreesboro, Tennessee, on the Western front, General Bragg launched a ferocious attack on the Army of the Cumberland, now under the command of General William S. Rosecrans. The Union army drove back the offensive, and Bragg's men were thus unable to prevent Federal advance toward Chattanooga.

The terrifying proportions that the conflict was assuming caused many citizens in the North to demand something more from the war than simply the restoration of the Union. Many began to think that if the Southern states did not want to return to the fold, they should be free to not do so, while others, instead, called for the war to bring the abolition of slavery.

Lincoln stated resolutely that fighting was solely for the sake of the Union and that the issue of slavery was little more than an inconvenience, which was entirely secondary to reunion. Nevertheless, toward the end of 1862, after the semi-victory at Antietam, the president had used his executive powers to issue a preliminary proclamation, whereby, as of January 1, slaves in the states still in rebellion against the government in Washington would be declared free. This proclamation was confirmed, as promised, on January 1, 1863, as the Emancipation Proclamation.

What are we to make of the Emancipation Proclamation? First and foremost, we must note that the proclamation was a purely executive order and thus required confirmation by legislative act, at which point, the president could have even been accused of exceeding his powers.

Legally, the proclamation was based on the principle whereby it is customary for any government to confiscate the assets of rebel subjects, and because there was no slavery in the North, slaves who were "confiscated" were ipso facto freed. Lincoln's decision was not, therefore, dictated by an ethical stance, nor did it constitute a political or idealistic agenda. Indeed, the proclamation explicitly stated that all "rebel" slaveholders who submitted by January 1, 1863, could retain their property. For the moment, all the pro-slavery states that had remained faithful to the Union were excluded from the emancipation, as well as the parts of the "rebel" states that had already been subdued.

The abolitionists attacked the proclamation vehemently, claiming that it only liberated slaves where Union forces were unable to enforce abolition and preserved slavery within the Union. But those who reasoned in this way failed to comprehend (or perhaps pretended not to understand) the true goal of the proclamation, which was essentially an act of civil war to help in bringing down the South. Others postulated (and not without a degree of accuracy) that the goal of the proclamation was to instigate bloody uprisings among the slaves of the South. If this was the case, the proclamation did not have its desired effect, as no such insurrections took place.

The proclamation was certainly in keeping with the total nature of the conflict. Throughout the North, industrial production was being pushed to the maximum; women were becoming increasingly involved in the production process to replace the tens of thousands of men being swallowed up by Moloch of war, and a law on conscription was being prepared that would eventually lead to the New York City draft riots of 1863.

Worse, still, was the social situation in the South. There, the industrial mobilization necessary to support the war effort had led to a shortage of fundamental items, such as food, medicine, paper, bandages, shoes, and other clothing. The blockade runners, who had begun to work increasingly for the armed forces, were unable to satisfy civilian needs as well. The Confederacy had naturally retaliated to the blockade, waging war on the Union's merchant shipping with the Confederate navy's convoy of cruisers. These raids proved an enormous success, heavily affecting Union trade and inflicting crippling damage on the United States Merchant Marine.

The year 1863 marked a clear and unavoidable shift in general strategy from the preceding year. The time for large-scale, simultaneous operations on all fronts was over; there were simply not enough troops or materials to allow it. It became evident that operations would be concentrated around the focal points that had proved decisive in the campaigns of 1862. All available forces would be deployed there, in an attempt to conclude the conflict through mass offensives of unheard of proportions.

These focal points could now be clearly defined: in the West, Vicksburg and the course of the Mississippi; in the center, Chattanooga and the fertile lands of Georgia; and in the east, Virginia, the "iron gate" of the Confederacy, in particular the Rapidan and Rappahannock rivers, which separated the two enemy armies.

The high command of the Confederacy remained firmly convinced that their forces should remain on the defensive and await the enemy's advance, but General Lee, as it would later emerge, was already plotting a decisive offensive.

In Virginia, Union General Burnside had been replaced, after the Fredericksburg fiasco, by General Joseph Hooker, also known as "Fighting Joe." A skilled commander of both division and corps, Hooker was aggressive and combative (and had thus earned his nickname) but was yet to prove himself worthy of independent command. It would not be long before it became clear just what type of commander he was.

Hooker had 138,000 men and over 400 cannons at his disposal, against Lee's 63,000 men and 220 guns. Lee had also been forced to send his best corps commander, General Longstreet, with two divisions and two artillery battalions, to North Carolina, to contain the enemy offensives that were being launched from Union bases along the coasts.

Like Burnside before him, Hooker had to cross the two rivers to engage with Lee's troops but did not want to commit the same mistake as his predecessor (and in this he proved successful). With a perfectly timed march, the bulk of the Army of the Potomac managed to cross the Rapidan well upstream of the Confederates, while three army corps, under Major General Sedgwick, were left facing the Confederates at Fredericksburg, as a ploy to deceive Lee. Hooker began his march on April 26, 1863, and, without firing a shot, managed to concentrate the bulk of his forces to flank Lee's troops, near the village of Chancellorsville.

Lee was not misled by such tactics. With the help of his skilled cavalry commander, General J. E. B. Stuart, Lee anticipated the Federal plan and moved most of his troops to confront Hooker, a counterattack of extraordinary foresight and audacity. Lee divided his troops, sending Stonewall Jackson's entire II Corps to carry out a brilliant flanking maneuver, which enveloped Hooker's unprotected right flank, while Lee confronted the Unionists (and the threat from Fredericksburg) with his own limited troops.

The operation was very successful. Hooker was caught completely off guard and suffered a heavy defeat, which forced him to withdraw back across the rivers in early May. Chancellorsville was perhaps Lee's most brilliant victory but also cost him dearly, as General Stonewall Jackson was mortally wounded by friendly fire during an expedition in the darkness of the forest.

Over on the Western theater, Grant had finally found a potential solution to the thorny problem of Vicksburg, the strategic Confederate stronghold. It had been handed to him on a plate by the Confederacy's enormous error in allowing the Mississippi River—which was particularly vulnerable to enemy penetration—to be the dividing line between the two sectors. Grant realized that if he were to proceed down the western shore of the great river, the Confederate forces of Louisiana stationed there would, in all likelihood, withdraw inland to defend deeper within their state. With the Confederates backing away from the river, Union troops would be able to reach Vicksburg downstream. In the meantime, Union ironclads, led by Rear Admiral David Dixon Porter, would force the passage at Vicksburg, to meet Grant's forces and carry them to the eastern shore. Even if things went according to plan, Grant would find himself behind the fortress, cut off from his rearguard. The plan was certainly extremely risky, but Grant was counting on the rich, local agriculture to provide enough food for his troops.

Grant had mobilized his troops as early as March 29. Moving the Union's entire Army of Tennessee, which consisted of some 43,000 men, down the right bank of the Mississippi River naturally proved a slow process; however, by April 26, Union forces had defeated and repulsed the Confederate forces along the river. Admiral Porter's squadron had run the Vicksburg batteries on April 16 and was waiting at the junction below to ferry Grant's forces across.

The campaign that followed was as sudden as it was devastating and has been aptly compared to Napoleon's Italian campaign of 1796. On May 1, at Port Gibson, Grant attacked and defeated General Bowen's Confederate forces (who nonetheless put up a resilient fight); a few days later, on May 12, he defeated Confederate General Gregg at Raymond, and finally, on the 14th, he captured Jackson, the state capital of Mississippi, sweeping away the Confederate forces stationed there.

On that same day, General Joseph Johnston arrived on the scene to take chief command of all Confederate forces operating in the field. Johnston's keen eye immediately spotted the danger: at his current rate, Grant would reach Vicksburg from the east, thus entirely isolating the stronghold, which would surely fall shortly after. Johnston believed that the only hope left would be for General Pemberton, commander of the Army of Mississippi, to immediately leave Vicksburg and, after converging with Johnston's men, concentrate all of his forces in the fight against Grant. If Grant was defeated, the city would remain in Confederate hands.

Unfortunately for the Confederates, Pemberton had no intention of obeying Johnston's sage advice. Meanwhile, through an informant, Grant had come into possession of a copy of Johnston's letter to Pemberton and decided to launch a lightning attack to capitalize on the enemy's hesitation. On May 16, he began his march on Vicksburg. As Pemberton faltered, Grant had attacked him and pushed him back inside Vicksburg.

Thus, the month of May 1863 proved decisive both in Virginia and in the West.

V

Lecture V

The spring and summer months of 1863 were critical to the outcome of the war. On the Western fronts, the fate of Vicksburg had been virtually sealed on May 16. After much hesitation, General Pemberton had finally decided to leave Vicksburg; contrary to Johnston's orders, however, he had left one-third of his forces inside the stronghold and thus had no more than 23,500 men and 90 cannons with him. Meanwhile, Johnston had been forced to surrender Jackson to the prevailing enemy forces, but, instead of moving east—as might have been expected—he had artfully and unexpectedly marched northwest (reproducing, on a smaller scale, General Mikhail Kutuzov's famous flank march against Napoleon in Moscow) so that his forces could join with Pemberton's, once the general had abandoned Vicksburg.

Pemberton, however, marched south with the intention of cutting Grant's (nonexistent) communication lines. Thus, the Union general, with a force of 33,000 men and 140 guns, pursued Pemberton's army and inflicted a convincing defeat at Champion Hill, on May 16. All Pemberton could do was retreat to the fortifications of Vicksburg, and on the 18th, Grant put the city under siege.

The fate of the Confederacy hinged upon Vicksburg, and the Confederate leaders in Richmond desperately sought a way to salvage the situation. The most logical proposal seemed to be that advanced by General Longstreet, Lee's best lieutenant: Lee would leave a limited number of troops in Virginia and head west with the bulk of his army, in an attempt to defeat Grant and save Vicksburg. After careful consideration, however, Lee decided against the plan and opted, instead, for a more offensive strategy: he would invade the North with his entire Army of Northern Virginia, in order to lure the enemy into a decisive battle and inflict a fatal blow.

A great deal has been written on the ensuing Gettysburg campaign, but historians have yet to provide a satisfactory answer as to why Lee turned down Longstreet's plan, which would have appeared the more effective, to gamble all on one mighty, but incredibly risky, campaign. The response given by many—which has rather unoriginally been adopted by the "politically correct" historians of today and their acolytes—is that, as a native of Virginia, Lee was largely uninterested in events on the other fronts.

A little careful study of Lee's correspondence is enough to reveal conclusively that Lee did not neglect the other fronts, nor had ever done so, and always contemplated the strategic situation as a whole. What, then, were the motives behind Lee's decision to launch an invasion?

The issue is a complex one and certainly warrants more thorough study. For the moment, we may advance a well-founded hypothesis, supported by the historical documents and sources: fundamentally, Lee had realized that time was running out for the Confederacy. Hence, a victory over Grant in the West would have forced the Union general to abandon the siege of Vicksburg and earned the South a moment's respite, but not much else. It was, in fact, highly unlikely that an offensive, under similar circumstances, would be able to wipe out the Union leader, and, in the best-case scenario, Longstreet's plan would have prolonged the conflict by another year—merely postponing the inevitable Union victory, given its numerical and industrial superiority.

The situation would, however, be rather different if Lee moved north into Maryland and Pennsylvania. Unlike Grant's men in the West, Union troops would not have the option of resorting to strategic retreat, as it would be inconceivable to leave cities such as Washington, Baltimore, Philadelphia (and perhaps even New York) in Confederate hands. The Union would thus be forced to concentrate all of its forces in one large defensive battle, and this would have given the Confederates a chance of outright victory.

If this was Lee's thinking (as indeed everything suggests that it was), his plan presents a fundamental flaw in its reliance on what was still a largely Napoleonic strategy at best and its complete disregard for the Industrial Revolution and how it had changed the course of the war. There is no doubt that the Army of Northern Virginia was one of the most formidable armies that the world had ever known, often appearing invincible in combat; indeed, half a century earlier, in the era of the smoothbore rifle and the bayonet, it would have destroyed anything in its path. But times had changed, and defense now prevailed over attack. Despite the fact that the Army of Northern Virginia's most brilliant victories—such as Fredericksburg and Chancellorsville—had all been defensive triumphs, Lee had failed to understand this, and Longstreet's legitimate insistence on an offensive strategy with defensive tactics went unheeded.

When, on July 1, 1863, the two armies clashed in Pennsylvania on the fields of Gettysburg, in a huge battle lasting three days, Lee had 80,000 men and 272 cannons at his disposal, against the 90,000 men and 366 cannons of the Union's General Meade. Lee's men showed resolve but were defeated, as every charge of the Confederate infantry was invariably met by the deadly fire of rifled guns. Eventually, the defense tactics wisely adopted by General George G. Meade, the new commander of the Army of the Potomac, got the better of the Confederates. On July 4, as the Army of Northern Virginia began its woeful retreat from Pennsylvania, Vicksburg—which was starving under siege—was forced to surrender unconditionally to General Ulysses Grant, leaving 30,000 prisoners, 15 generals, and 260 cannons to Union forces.

Whatever has been written about it, the Battle of Gettysburg was as decisive to the outcome of the Civil War as the Battle of Waterloo was to the Napoleonic Wars. But while the French forces lost all desire to fight for Napoleon and were ready to throw in the towel after Waterloo, the Civil War was able to continue as the Southern nation was resolved to fight to the death. For this reason, President Davis rejected the letter of resignation that Lee promptly sent him. Without a doubt, though, the defeats at Gettysburg and Vicksburg had cost the Confederacy all hope of winning the war; at best, it could still avoid defeat, by wearing down the enemy and negotiating a peace of compromise.

To make matters worse, the surrender of Vicksburg had irreparably severed the Confederacy in two. Wasting no time at all, Union General Rosecrans pushed General Bragg out of Chattanooga and advanced threateningly into Georgia. The South met this impending danger with a surge of pride: Lee sent General Longstreet and his army corps west to join with General Bragg's men, bringing Confederate forces to a total of 73,000 men and 198 cannons, and at Chickamauga, they won a resounding victory over Rosecrans's 68,000 men.

The Union reacted readily, and General George Thomas replaced Rosecrans at the head of the Army of the Cumberland. A Virginian slaveholder who had remained faithful to the Union, Thomas had proved instrumental in preserving the Union army from complete destruction at Chickamauga. The Union's Army of Tennessee, then under the command of General Sherman, was immediately sent to reinforce the Army of the Cumberland, and a corps of the Army of the Potomac, led by Joseph Hooker, arrived from the east. Grant assumed supreme command of all fronts in the West, and, on November 25, he defeated Bragg and took Chattanooga, renewing the Union threat on Georgia.

Thus, in 1863, the Confederacy tried to deal a devastating blow to the Union and failed. Although the situation appeared desperate, all hope had not been lost, and the Confederate leaders in Richmond were boldly preparing to play the few cards they still had left. Indeed, it was now the Union's turn to want to act quickly: although it could seemingly rely on inexhaustible human, material, and military resources, 1864 was, after all, an election year. In November, citizens of the Union would be called to the polls to elect a new president, as domestic unrest over the war was growing steadily by the day. The conflict had grown more brutal and bloody than anyone could have imagined: entire generations were being swallowed up by the front lines; the hospitals were overflowing with the injured, sick, and dying; and the costs of war had become almost unbearable. Advocating disengagement and surrender, the "pro-peace" party would have tried desperately to prevent the public from reelecting Lincoln—who, in turn, would have had no chance of victory without a substantial success on the front lines.

The situation in the South was certainly far more tragic, but the impending threat of the Union armies meant that (barring few exceptions) the Southerners were willing to grit their teeth and accept all sacrifice. And with the South willing to fight to the death, who would be able to secure the victories that the Union needed to avoid an imminent crisis? On March 9, 1864, General Ulysses Grant—who had recently been made lieutenant general (a rank only previously held by George Washington)—assumed command of all the Union armies, as Halleck agreed to be demoted to chief of staff.

Grant devised a clear strategy for the campaign of 1864, which consisted in crushing all the Confederate forces in a huge, two-pronged pincer movement. One prong—made up of the Army of the Potomac, led by General Meade, and Burnside's IX Army Corps, both under Grant's direct control—would move south into Virginia, where Grant would establish his headquarters; the other prong—composed of the Armies of the Cumberland, Tennessee, and Ohio—would cut through Georgia under the command of General Sherman.

In Virginia, the Union troops would take on Lee's Army of Northern Virginia, while, in Georgia, they would face the Confederate Army of Tennessee, under the command of another skilled leader, General Joseph E. Johnston. The two prongs of the attack had to move simultaneously, to prevent the Confederates from using their internal lines of communications, as they had done successfully at Chickamauga. Overall, about 350,000 men would take part in the Unionist offensive, while the Confederates could count on approximately 200,000. The Confederates were still a formidable force to be reckoned with, made up of brave and able fighters, who were still in good spirits, and military leaders of the highest order.

Grant's prodigious operation began on all fronts at midnight on May 3, 1864. An aerial perspective of the execution of Grant's strategy reveals a substantial difference in how the plan was carried out on the two major fronts of Virginia and Georgia. Interestingly, the divergences reflect the different personalities of the Confederate leaders operating on the two fronts.

Lee, for one, remained faithful to the Napoleonic system of war; indeed, the Virginia campaign of 1864 presents a number of analogies with Napoleon's admirable campaign of France in 1814. Maintaining his aggressive tactics, Lee decided to attack Grant immediately, as soon as Union forces crossed the Rapidan River, and the Union general also intended to launch an immediate offensive against the Confederates; thus, when the two sides engaged, the terrible and bloody Battle of the Wilderness ensued. The battle ended as a stalemate but provided the two military leaders with a chance to size up their respective opponent.

Grant's aggressiveness and determination certainly impressed Lee, and, from then onward, the Confederate leader adopted a much more guarded approach when confronting his rival, fighting mainly on the defensive and aiming to protect all routes to Richmond. Grant, in turn, focused primarily on two strategic priorities. First, he aimed to sever Lee's lines of communication, which would force the Confederate leader to expose Richmond, placing him in a similar situation to that in which General Meade had defended Pennsylvania in 1863. Grant thus hoped that, faced with a potential threat on the Confederate capital, Lee would be lured into fight under unfavorable conditions. Secondly, he intended to attack Lee directly whenever he had the chance, in an attempt to wear down his forces (as Grant knew that, unlike the Union, the Confederacy could rely on limited human resources).

The military genius of the two opponents was evident from the outset of the campaign. After the bloodshed of the Battle of the Wilderness, both sides wondered what Grant's next move would be. When lesser generals—such as Hooker or Burnside—might have crossed back over the Rapidan River, to regroup and catch their breath, Grant ordered his men to march on—not northward, in retreat, but southward, right to the heart of the enemy—and the Union troops met the command with enthusiasm.

Grant's first territorial objective was the vital crossroads at Spotsylvania. Possession of Spotsylvania would have granted a critical advantage to the Union troops and would have left Lee at a strong tactical disadvantage. The brilliant Southern leader, however, guessed the enemy's intentions, and when Union forces reached Spotsylvania, they found the Confederates manning the crossroads. Lee had thus prevented Grant from cutting his lines of communication and was keeping all routes to the Confederate capital well defended.

Much like Napoleon in 1814, Lee was well aware that his strategy came at a price, as enemy troops were drawing closer to Richmond by the day. The Confederate leader feared a siege on the capital, which would have made surrender only a matter of time.

Lee found himself, however, with few other options. Grant had launched two subsidiary attacks in an attempt to capitalize on the Union forces' numerical superiority: one army corps operated along the Shenandoah valley (but was defeated by the Confederates in the Battle of New Market—thanks, partly, to the participation of the young cadets of the Virginia Military Institute), while, on the other side of Richmond, the Army of the James served along the James River, intercepting communications between the Confederate capital and the strategic rail hub of Petersburg (and thus the rest of the South). Thankfully for the Confederates, General Beauregard, who had been hastily called from Charleston, succeeded in gathering enough forces to halt the Union advance (led by General Benjamin Butler) at a good distance from Petersburg.

The two armies attempted to engage each other, with some of the most brilliant attacks and counterattacks in the history of warfare, and a confrontation took place on May 31 at Cold Harbor, over the same ground where they had fought in 1862. Lee had once again managed to interpose his troops between the Confederate capital and Grant's divisions, but the Confederate troops now had Richmond directly behind them and nowhere else to withdraw to. Nevertheless, they managed to repulse Grant's frontal assault, with heavy losses on both sides.

Grant was not, however, one to give up easily. On May 13, taking Lee completely by surprise, Union forces suddenly crossed the James, by constructing a huge pontoon bridge, and invaded Petersburg. Fortunately for the Confederates, General Beauregard arrived just in time to defend the city, but Lee's fear—that Grant would force him into a siege—was about to become a reality. Union forces closed in along the sixty kilometers of trenches protecting Richmond and Petersburg, while Grant began a long-term flanking maneuver to cut the rail lines that connected the two cities with the rest of the South.

The situation was very different on the Georgian front, due, partly, to the different dispositions of Generals Johnston and Sherman. Johnston had immediately recognized the enemy's substantial numerical superiority and, unlike Lee, had decided not to attack. The Confederate general knew very well that an offensive would be precisely what Sherman was hoping for—and had instead decided, as the fundamental objective of his strategy, to keep his army intact and patiently await the moment to deal a devastating blow. Johnston thus aimed to yield ground (as slowly as possible) in order to buy time. In the campaign of 1864, he proved to be a real master of the tactical retreat and deserves to be remembered alongside such military leaders as Fabius Maximus, Raimondo Montecuccoli, Turenne, and Albert Kesselring.

Having sized up his enemy, Sherman responded to Johnston's tactics by exploiting the numerical superiority of his Union troops to conduct a series of enveloping maneuvers. Johnston, however, would time his withdrawal to perfection, and his troops would take up new positions, which they would immediately defend with trenches and land fortifications, making frontal assault useless.

The trench—a new and devastating addition to the battlefield—had become a vital part of conflict by the campaign of 1864 (featuring, less frequently, in certain battles of the year before). As defense had begun to prevail over attack, both sides had increasingly begun to dig trenches; indeed, many combatants mention in their letters from the front lines that throughout the entire campaign, and even the bloodiest battles, they were never able to see their enemies—just the trenches from which they fired.

After another advance, on June 19, Sherman's troops once again engaged Johnston's forces, who on this occasion were formidably entrenched along the Kennesaw Mountains, the last Confederate bastion before Atlanta. Thus, with his cunning strategy, "Old Joe" (as his soldiers affectionately called him) had actually delayed Sherman's march toward Atlanta more than Lee had hindered Grant. Furthermore, Johnston had preserved his army virtually intact, suffering only negligible losses. Exasperated by Johnston's dilatory tactics, Sherman eventually decided to launch a frontal assault on June 27, which predictably ended in failure and very heavy casualties.

The two leaders resumed their duel of flank and counter-flank maneuvers after the Battle of Kennesaw Mountain, and, by July 17, Johnston found himself in a similar position to that occupied by Lee, one month before, at Cold Harbor—with his men forming a defensive line behind the Chattahoochee River and Peachtree Creek and with the fortifications of Atlanta directly behind them.

What would happen next? Johnston's delaying tactics had been successful and had preserved his army, which was ready for battle. "I can hold Atlanta forever," Johnston is purported to have declared (although the sources are contradictory)—and it seems that, using Atlanta as his base, he intended to defend the city in much the same way as Lee was operating in Richmond and Petersburg.

But Johnston's tactical retreat had proved costly to the Confederacy, and the industrial center of Rome, Georgia, along with much Confederate territory, had been lost. Johnston's enemies (and there were several) began to voice their criticism of the general, and on that same July 17, President Davis took the drastic (and misguided) decision to replace Johnston with General John Bell Hood. He could not have made a more calamitous decision.

Hood knew only one strategy: attack. He had a reputation for his aggressiveness, and his offensive tactics favored unrelenting attack, with little heed to enemy strength and numbers. The Confederate soldiers of the Army of Tennessee, who were well aware of this and had no confidence in Hood, asked in vain for "Old Joe" to be reinstated.

Under new command, the Confederates immediately went on the attack. The two Battles of Atlanta and the Battle of Ezra Church ensued; both ended inconclusively. By the time the fighting was over, the Army of Tennessee had lost 15,000 men, either killed or wounded. An even bigger blow had been dealt to the Confederate cause, as Atlanta had become untenable, and the city was evacuated on September 2, leaving it in enemy hands.

Thus, Lincoln had finally secured the important victory he needed. Although the Democrats had recently nominated ex-general McClellan as their "pacifist" candidate, the conquest of Atlanta swept away any hopes he may have entertained of being elected, and contributed powerfully to Lincoln's reelection. The Western front had, once again, proved to be the Confederacy's undoing.

More was yet to come, though, as Sherman began his famous march through Georgia, destroying everything that lay in his path. Hood tried in vain to fight back by invading Tennessee, but Sherman sent the reliable Major General George H. Thomas, with the Army of the Cumberland, in pursuit, and they destroyed Hood's forces in the two bloody battles of Franklin and Nashville. After the Tennessee debacle, General Hood resigned. As the year drew to its end, Sherman's troops captured the large Confederate port of Savannah, where they connected with the Union navy fleet on December 21. In Virginia, Lee had detached his II Army Corps and—just as Stonewall Jackson had done before him—had been conducting several intimidating operations in the direction of Washington, through the Shenandoah valley. However, Grant sent General Philip Sheridan to the valley, and the Union general convincingly defeated the Confederates at Cedar Creek and destroyed the valley's economic infrastructure, so that it could no longer be used by as a Confederate base of operations.

As the year 1865 began, Sherman left Savannah to march northward, through the Carolinas, in the direction of Grant's men, destroying everything in his path. President Davis resorted to extreme measures to deal with the impending threat and appointed Lee general in chief of all Confederate forces. As his first move, the Virginian recalled Joseph Johnston to take command of what was left of the Army of Tennessee after its unfortunate spell under General Hood. "Old Joe" wasted no time and went on the offensive. He had noticed that Sherman's forces were advancing in widely scattered columns and intended to attack one column in an attempt to overpower it before the other columns could arrive as reinforcements. After initial success at Averasboro, Johnston was able to catch an isolated wing of Sherman's army by surprise at Bentonville, North Carolina, on March 19 and 20. Johnston was on the verge of defeating the Federal unit when Sherman's reinforcements arrived in all haste, and the Confederate leader was made to retreat.

Meanwhile, over in Virginia, Grant had cut the last rail line still connecting Richmond with the rest of the South, forcing Lee to evacuate the capital. Lee still had a final card up his sleeve and marched west and then south, in an attempt to join with Johnston's troops and together give battle to Sherman. Grant was set on not letting Lee escape—and, while the Army of the Potomac, led by Meade, was hot on Lee's heels, he dispatched General Sheridan, with his cavalry corps, to pursue the Confederate forces and cut them off from the front. Thus, at the beginning of April 1865, Lee found himself cornered at Appomattox Court House. All his desperate efforts to break the Union's vice-like grip were in vain, and on April 9, 1865, he was forced to surrender to Grant, who offered very generous terms. Johnston's forces capitulated to Sherman a few days later at Bennett's Farm, in North Carolina.

The war was over, but one final, tragic event was yet to come. On April 14, President Lincoln was assassinated in obscure circumstances. The wider ramifications of the conspiracy have yet to be certainly established, and perhaps never will be. At the time, and for good reason, public outcry pinned the murder on a Southern plot, and Confederate President Jefferson Davis was thrown in jail and chained like a criminal, in a futile attempt to lay the blame on him. Lincoln's killer, John Wilkes Booth—a theater actor with flagrant Southern sympathies—was pursued, captured, and killed; his mouth, therefore, remained shut forever. The more extremist factions of the Republican Party in power took advantage of the murder to "wave the bloody toga," as Anthony had done at Caesar's funeral, and impose a brutal, "Carthaginian peace"—which, as the documents confirm, is precisely what Lincoln wanted to avoid.

Nowadays, a different view of the assassination has begun to emerge. It has been pointed out that, for all his Southern sympathies, Booth had never actually left Washington, never visited the Confederacy, and never volunteered to fight for its cause. It appears, furthermore, that Booth had obscure contacts with Federal espionage, and this would lead us to suspect that he was acting as agent provocateur on behalf of one such organization and that someone—certainly not in the South—had recruited him to remove the president, whose policies had become a source of great annoyance in certain circles. With Lincoln out of the picture, it would have been easier to spread an attitude of moral lynching with regard to the South, which was fundamental for this "Carthaginian peace" to be imposed.

What were Lincoln's postwar plans, and why did they incense these extremist groups within his own party? Essentially, Lincoln believed that the South could not and should not be treated as a defeated enemy but rather as a prodigal brother who had returned to the family, after a spell of absence. Lincoln believed that slavery could not be regarded as the South's fault—if anything, responsibility lay with the entire Union; therefore, if one-third of the electorate in the secessionist states were to vote to repeal the ordinance of secession and accept the Thirteenth Amendment of the Constitution (which abolished slavery outright, overriding the legally precarious Emancipation Proclamation), these states would once again become full members of the Union. When it came to the issue of slavery, Lincoln intended the Thirteenth Amendment as programmatic, rather than mandatory, and thus believed that the victorious states should be made to pay a large sum (around 400 million dollars) to the Southern states as compensation for the abolition of slavery—a kind of Marshall Plan of its time.

Lincoln's plans died with him, and the Republican extremists prevailed. The South was subjected to a harsh military occupation and treated as if it were an enemy land that had been subdued by force. Needless to say, no compensation was offered for the emancipation of slaves. In fact, the Southern citizens, even the most humble—and in particular the class of plantation owners—suffered a much more radical expropriation than the nobility and clergy had done in the French Revolution. Confederate money was declared worthless, the Confederacy's debt was voided, slavery was abolished without compensation, and all those who had taken up arms against the Union (almost all male Southerners) were deprived of the right to vote. This terrible "era of reconstruction" ended only in 1876, but the South was reduced to poverty for several decades.

Although the South was made to bear more of the economic burden, the cost of the war had been huge for the entire Union, amounting to over ten billion dollars. And the cost in human lives was even greater. The Union had lost 365,205 men, with 285,245 wounded or mutilated; the Confederacy had approximately 200,000 dead and 150,000 wounded or mutilated. Overall, more than a million were killed or wounded—an appalling figure in itself, which, in some cases, exceeds the percentage of loss of life in World War I (in which, for example, Italy lost 600,000 men, out of a population of about 30 million; while, in the Civil War, the South lost 200,000 men out of a population of 5 million—which, in percentage terms, is more than double).

In the South, in particular, an entire generation had been wiped out, and losses were just as horrific in the North. The South, however, also had to deal with the enormous damage done to property and infrastructure, as its bridges, roads, railways, and telegraph lines had been almost entirely destroyed. The huge wastage of Southern livestock contributed significantly to the spread of diseases of poverty, such as intestinal parasites and pellagra.

On the economic front, the North's industrial and financial elite had gained the upper hand, as an ad valorem duty of over 47 percent was introduced, ensuring a system of total protectionism. Another measure, known as the Homestead Act, had also been approved, opening up the entire West for settlement by anyone who had not fought against the Union. This westward expansion was one of the contributing causes of the American Indian Wars that lasted until 1890.

What, then, was the positive outcome of the conflict (assuming that war can ever have a positive outcome)? The abolition of slavery is certainly not the answer to this question. Lincoln firmly believed that fighting a war to eliminate slavery was madness and had prepared a plan for the peaceful abolition of the "peculiar institution" by 1900. The United States would thus have resembled Brazil, where slavery died out peacefully toward the end of the century. Besides, in the final stages of the Civil War, the Confederacy had passed a law whereby those slaves who fought voluntarily for the South would have obtained freedom, Confederate citizenship, and a piece of land. Lincoln had issued the Emancipation Proclamation as a civil-war measure, and it had taken the Thirteenth Amendment to legalize the proclamation, which was purely an executive act. The Union did use the struggle against slavery as an ideological weapon, as the war became increasingly brutal, and there was the risk that certain European nations might recognize the Confederacy, but this was merely wartime propaganda.

Lincoln made his political outlook very clear, on several occasions: the war would decide whether the United States would become "one nation or two." He envisioned a "great Republic," a harmonious union, rather than the tangle of *disjecta membra* the country had been until that point. From this point of view, the political figure whom Lincoln most resembles is Otto von Bismarck. In the same way as the "Iron Chancellor" unified Germany, transforming the old confederation into a unitary state (on a federal basis), the great president fought victoriously for the birth of the American nation. In this light, comparison to Cavour is also justified.

The political and military movement led by Lincoln can thus be situated within the larger framework of nineteenth-century nationalism and its idea of the nation-state. As Bismarck acutely observed to Grant (when the American general visited Germany after the war), the unification of America was also achieved "by blood and iron." Those who had opposed unification were men of the past, who were completely detached from the modern notion of the nation-state. When Robert Edward Lee, who opposed both secession and slavery, was asked by General Scott to take command of the Union army, he replied: "I cannot bear arms against my state." Lee's allegiance was to Virginia first and then to his country. Was this not a radically different view from that of, say, Bismarck, Cavour—or Lincoln?

The nineteenth century was the century of nationality; there was no place for criticism of nationalism. It would have seemed difficult to believe that the modern nation-state has, in many ways, proven to be a myth (and a dangerous one, at that—if we consider its role in triggering the world wars).

There was, however, another side to Lincoln that distinguished him from his European colleagues. Bismarck strongly desired a liberal state; Cavour a parliamentary one; Lincoln, however, aspired to something more. Much like Giuseppe Mazzini, he believed that the "great Republic" of the United States should offer the world a model of democracy. He believed it profoundly undemocratic that a party, or a people, defeated by vote, should abandon parliament rather than adapt to the vote. Such flagrant disregard for the principles of democracy would confirm the beliefs of the military monarchies of Europe, with their claims that the public was unable to govern itself.

For this reason, he also conceived the Civil War as a struggle for democracy. As such, a democratic government had to prove it was capable of quashing a rebellion by using force, while preserving democracy. The president believed that this would salvage the principle of democracy in the world (as he clearly stated in his Gettysburg Address) and that the United States would therefore be able to intervene in its defense, should democracy be threatened in Europe. Lincoln thus anticipated—with incredible foresight— the policy that Franklin, Roosevelt, and Truman would subsequently adopt to deal with totalitarian regimes of the twentieth century and the threats they posed.

This was, in many respects, Lincoln's most influential idea, and it largely disqualifies the counterargument that, for the South, the United States was not a "great Republic" but a union of independent and sovereign states, each of which retained the right to leave the union, should its interests be damaged. Of course, these two different ways of conceiving the Union were mutually exclusive: the conflict was resolved on the battlefields, by the force of arms. For better or for worse, one side lost and was eliminated; the other won.

Thus, the Civil War molded modern America and foretold its destiny. In its postwar development, the United States followed the general direction of the rest of the Western world at that time. The Industrial Revolution undoubtedly benefitted massively from this course of events, as the country was stably transformed into a single national market. One of the victims of this process was the South's particularism, which was swept away along with any opposition to a central banking system, protectionist tariffs, and the large-scale investment of capital to facilitate industrial development.

It took years before any sort of moderation was introduced to restrict the overwhelming supremacy of the large industrial and financial groups, but a different question remains to be answered. Did the Civil War impede or promote economic progress? Undoubtedly, the removal of Southern opposition did away with a huge obstacle to economic development, as the abolition of slavery strengthened the labor market by creating a huge "industrial reserve army." At the current state of research, however, more cannot be said on the matter, but I expect the debate among economic historians to continue for a long time.

Further Readings

PREMISE

For many years, literature in Italian on the American Civil War was virtually nonexistent. Italian historians largely ignored the problem, and readers had to make do with such novels as *Uncle Tom's Cabin*, which portray events in an evidently distorted way. Nowadays, the situation has finally changed, with the publication in 1966 of my *Storia della guerra civile americana* (*History of the American Civil War*) acting as a turning point. The short bibliographic essay that follows recommends a number of books that may be of interest to any reader aspiring to a more comprehensive study of the issue. The list is divided by subheadings and includes works written both in English and Italian.

GENERAL WORKS

History of the United States

Luraghi, Raimondo. *Gli Stati Uniti* [The United States]. Turin: Utet, 1974.
Tindall, George B. *America: A Narrative History*. New York: Norton, 1984.

The American Civil War

Catton, Bruce. *The Centennial History of the Civil War*. 3 vols. New York: Doubleday, 1961.
Luraghi, Raimondo, ed. *La Guerra Civile Americana* [The American Civil War]. Bologna: Il Mulino, 1978. In this book, a number of essays written by some of the most prominent experts on the Civil War have been translated and collected—together with a my long

introductory essay, in which certain aspects of my book *History of the American Civil War* are revisited and addressed more fully.

———. *Storia della Guerra Civile Americana* [History of the American Civil War]. 6th ed. Milan: BUR, 1994.

Randall, J. G., and D. Donald. *The Civil War and Reconstruction.* Lexington, MA: Heath, 1969.

THE CRISIS IN THE UNION

In addition to the works mentioned above, see:

Craven, Avery O. *Civil War in the Making.* Baton Rouge: Louisiana State University Press, 1959.
———. *The Coming of the Civil War.* Chicago: University of Chicago Press, 1957.
———. *The Irrepressible Conflict, 1850–1865.* New York: Scholarly Press, 1934.

SLAVERY

Davis, David B. *The Problem of Slavery in Western Cultures.* Ithaca, NY: Cornell University Press, 1966.
Genovese, Eugene D. *The Political Economy of Slavery.* Middletown, CT: Wesleyan University Press, 1961.
———. *Roll, Jordan, Roll: The World the Slaves Made.* New York: Random House, 1974.
Luraghi, Raimondo. "Wage Labor in the 'Rice Belt' of Northern Italy and Slave Labor in the American South: A First Approach." *Southern Studies* 16, no. 2 (Summer 1977): 109–27.
Phillips, Ulrich B. *American Negro Slavery.* Edited by Eugene D. Genovese. Baton Rouge: Louisiana State University Press, 1966. Any in-depth study of the issue should start with this outdated, but still excellent, work.

AFRICAN AMERICAN HISTORY

Ginzburg Migliorino, Ellen. *La Marcia Immobile: Storia dei neri americani dal 1770 al 1970* [The Motionless March: History of Black Americans from 1770 to 1970]. Milan: Selene, 1994.
Jordan, Winthrop D. *White over Black: American Attitude toward the Negro, 1550–1812.* Chapel Hill: University of North Carolina Press, 1968.

THE OLD SOUTH

Genovese, Eugene D. *The World the Slaveholders Made.* Middletown, CT: Wesleyan University Press, 1960.
Luraghi, Raimondo. *The Rise and Fall of the Plantation South.* New York: New Viewpoints, 1978.

Political Ideology of the Old South

Cash, Wilbur J. *The Mind of the South.* New York: Vintage Books, 1941.

The Greatest Antebellum Southern "Ideologue"

Calhoun, John C. *A Disquisition on Government*. South Bend, IN: St. Augustine's Press, 2007.
Salvadori, Massimo. *Potere e Libertà nel Mondo modern: John Calhoun: un genio imbarazzante* [Power and Freedom in the Modern World: John Calhoun: An Embarrassing Genius]. Bari: Laterza, 1996.

National Identity in the South

Carpenter, Jesse T. *The South as a Conscious Minority*. Gloucester, MA: Peter Smith, 1963.
Craven, Avery O. *The Growth of Southern Nationalism, 1848–1861*. Baton Rouge: Louisiana State University Press, 1953.
Luraghi, Raimondo. "The Civil War and the Modernization of American Society: Social Structure and Industrial Revolution in the Old South before and during the War." In *Civil War History*, 18 (1972):230–50.
———. "Il sud degli Stati Uniti fino alla guerra civile" [The South before the Civil War]. In *Università degli Studi di Genova: Annali della Facoltà di Scienze Politiche*, 11–13 (1983–86):141.
———. "The United States South: Region or Nation?" In *The United States South: Regionalism and Identity*, edited by V. Gennaro Leirda and T. Westendorp, 1. Rome: Bulzoni, 1991.

THE LINCOLN PRESIDENCY

The best biography of Lincoln is still:

Thomas, Benjamin. *Abraham Lincoln: A Biography*. Carbondale: Southern Illinois University Press, 1952.

Also excellent:

Randall, James G., and Richard N. Current. *Lincoln the President*. 4 vols. New York: Dodd, Mead, 1945.

On a particular issue:

Luraghi, Raimondo. "Il Liberalismo di Lincoln" [Lincoln's Liberalism]. In *Miscellanea in Onore di Ruggero Moscati*, 589. Naples: Edizioni Scientifiche Italiane, 1985.

THE CONFEDERATE STATES OF AMERICA

The best books on the subject remain:

Coulter, E. Merton. *The Confederate States of America, 1861–1865*. Baton Rouge: Louisiana State University Press, 1950.
Roland, Charles P. *The Confederacy*. Chicago: University of Chicago Press, 1960.
Thomas, Emory M. *The Confederate Nation, 1861–1865*. New York: Harper Perennial, 1979.
Vandiver, Frank I. *Their Tattered Flags: The Epic of the Confederacy*. College Station: Texas A&M University Press, 1970.

See also:

Luraghi, Raimondo. "Appunti sulla Storiografia degli Stati Confederati d'America" [Notes on the Historiography of the Confederate States of America]. In *Università degli Studi di Genova: Annali della Facoltà di Scienze Politiche*, 1 (1973):149.

———. "La finanza bellica e l'industrializzazione degli Stati Confederati d'America durante la Guerra Civile americana, 1861–1865" [Finance and Industrialization of the Confederate States of America during the American Civil War, 1861–1865]. In *Fra Spazio e Tempo: Studi in onore di Luigi de Rosa*, 2 (1995):657. Naples.

———. "Origini e struttura della Costituzione degli Stati Confederati d'America" [Origins and Structure of the Constitution of the Confederate States of America]. In *Studi Americani*, 16 (1970):151–63.

BIOGRAPHIES

Apart from the books on Lincoln mentioned above, the most authoritative are the following:

Robert E. Lee

The best biography is still the classic:

Freeman, Douglas S. *Robert E. Lee: A Biography*. 4 vols. New York: Charles Scribner's Sons, 1934

To which we must add:

Freeman, Douglas S. *Lee's Lieutenants: A Study in Command*. 3 vols.

Ulysses S. Grant

A fully satisfactory biography is yet to be written. However, for his military career, the best remains:

Fuller, J. F. C. *The Generalship of Ulysses Grant*. Bloomington: Indiana University Press, 1958.

Confederate President Jefferson F. Davis

Also lacking a fully satisfactory biography, the most acceptable is:

Davis, William C. *Jefferson Davis: The Man and His Hour*. Baton Rouge: Louisiana State University Press, 1991.

General Thomas Jonathan "Stonewall" Jackson

There are the excellent:

Henderson, G. F. R. *Stonewall Jackson and the American Civil War*. London: McKay, 1961.
Vandiver, Frank I. *Mighty Stonewall*. New York: McGraw Hill, 1957.

General Sherman

On this controversial figure, there are three excellent biographical works:

Lewis, Lloyd. *Sherman, Fighting Prophet*. New York: Harcourt Brace, 1958.
Liddel Hart, Sir Basil H. *Sherman: Soldier, Realist, American*. New York: Praeger, 1958.
Marszalek, John S. *Sherman: A Soldier's Passion for Order*. Carbondale: Southern Illinois University Press, 1994.

General James Longstreet

Piston, William G. *Lee's Tarnished General: James Longstreet and Southern History*. Athens: University of Georgia Press, 1987.
Wert, Jeffry D. *Longstreet*. New York: Simon and Schuster, 1993.

General Joseph E. Johnston

Symonds, Craig L. *Joseph E. Johnston: Civil War Biography*. New York: Norton, 1992.

General Pierre G. T. Beauregard

Williams, T. Harry. *Beauregard: Napoleon in Gray*. Baton Rouge: Louisiana State University Press, 1955.

General Nathan B. Forrest

Henry, Robert S. *First with the Most: Nathan Bedford Forrest*. Indianapolis: Bobs-Merrill, 1944.

John Brown

On this controversial figure:

Schenone, Giulio. *John Brown: l'Apostolo degli schiavi* [John Brown: The Apostle of Slaves]. Milan: Mursia, 1984.

THE CIVIL WAR CAMPAIGNS

Bearss, Edwin C. *The Campaign for Vicksburg*. 3 vols. Dayton, OH: Morningside House, 1985.
Bigelow, John Bigelow. *The Campaign of Chancellorsville: A Strategic and Tactical Study*. New Haven, CT: Yale University Press, 1919.
Coddington, Edwin B. *The Gettysburg Campaign: A Study in Command*. New York: Charles Scribner's Sons, 1968.
Johnston, R. M. *Bull Run: Its Strategy and Tactics*. Boston: Houghton Mifflin, 1913.
Luraghi, Raimondo. "Le Guerre del Risorgimento e la Guerra tra gli Stati americani: la rivoluzione tecnologica, logistica, tattica e strategica" [The Wars of the Risorgimento and the American Civil War: Technological, Logistic, Tactical and Strategic Revolutions]. In *Italia e Stati Uniti nell'Età del Risorgimento e della Guerra Civile*, 213–37. Florence: La Nuova Italia, 1969.
———. "La grande strategia della Guerra Civile americana e l'avvento della guerra totale" [The Great Strategy of the American Civil War and the Advent of Total War]. *Revue Internationale d'Histoire Militaire* 39 (1978): 290–321.

——. "Guerre Civile Américaine et Alliances Etrangères. Les 'quasi-alliances' europeenes pendant la guerre de secession (1861–1865)." In *Forces Armees et Systèmes d'Alliance*, 369. Montpellier, 1981.

McDonough, James L. *Stones River—Bloody Winter in Tennessee*. Knoxville: University of Tennessee Press, 1980.

Meredith, R. *Storm over Sumter*. New York: Simon and Schuster, 1957.

Sears, Stephen W. *Landscape Turned Red: The Battle of Antietam*. New York: Tichnor and Fields, 1983.

——. *To the Gates of Richmond: The Peninsula Campaign*. New York: Houghton Mifflin, 1983.

Steere, Edward. *The Wilderness Campaign*. New York: Stackpole, 1960.

Sword, Wiley. *Shiloh: Bloody April*. New York: Morrow, 1974.

Tucker, Glenn. *Chickamauga: Bloody Battle in the West*. Dayton, OH: Morningside, 1961.

Hennessey, John J. *Return to Bull Run*. New York: Simon and Schuster, 1993.

THE CIVIL WAR AT SEA

Luraghi, Raimondo. *A History of the Confederate Navy*. Annapolis, MD, 1996.

Appendix

Data on certain decisive battles in history

Battle	Forces deployed
Arbela, 331 BC	Macedonians, 47,000
	Persians, 245,000
Zama, 202 BC	Romans and allies, 43,000
	Carthaginians, 49,000
Pharsalus, 48 BC	Caesarians, 28,000
	Pompeians, 37,000
Waterloo, 1815	British and allies, 68,000
	Prussians, 89,000
	French, 72,000
Gettysburg, 1863	Unionist, 90,000
	Confederate, 80,000

About the Author

Raimondo Luraghi is professor emeritus of American history at the University of Genoa and honorary member of the Italian Association of Canadian Studies and the Italian Association of North American Studies. He is honorary president of the Italian Society of Military History, Italian representative in the International Commission on Comparative Military History, president of the Scientific Committee of the Italian Association of Military Volunteers, and a member of the American Society for Military History and the U.S. Naval Institute. He is considered one of the greatest European authorities on the American Civil War.